DOROTHY DAY

DOROTHY DAY

Friend to the Forgotten

Deborah Kent

William B. Eerdmans Publishing Company
Grand Rapids, Michigan / Cambridge, U.K.

© 1996 Wm. B. Eerdmans Publishing Co.
255 Jefferson Ave. S.E., Grand Rapids, Michigan 49503 /
P.O. Box 163, Cambridge CB2 9PU U.K.

Printed in the United States of America

01 00 99 98 97 96   7 6 5 4 3 2 1

Library of Congress Cataloging-in-Publication Data

Kent, Deborah.
Dorothy Day : friend to the forgotten / Deborah Kent.
p.   cm.
ISBN 0-8028-5117-7 (hardcover : alk paper).
ISBN 0-8028-5100-2 (paperback : alk paper).
1. Day, Dorothy, 1897-1980.   2. Catholic converts —
United States — Biography.   3. Women social reformers —
United States — Biography.
I. Title.
BX4705.D283K46   1996
267'.182'092 — dc20
[B]   95-47719
                                        CIP

The author and the publisher gratefully acknowledge permission to quote excerpts from *The Long Loneliness* by Dorothy Day. Copyright © 1952 by Harper & Row, Publishers, Inc. Copyright renewed © 1980 by Tamar Teresa Hennessy. Reprinted by permission of HarperCollins Publishers, Inc.

Contents

Prologue: To Overcome Evil with Good   vii

1. A Family Apart   1

2. To Change the World   15

3. Adrift   29

4. The Cottage by the Sea   44

5. A Prayer and an Answer   56

6. A Penny a Copy   66

7. House of Hospitality   76

8. Back to the Land   86

9. The Troubled Path of Peace   95

10. The End of an Era   109

11. The Challenge of Change   119

12. The End of the Pilgrimage   128

Epilogue: A Legacy of Love   135

My Sources for This Book   138

Suggestions for Further Reading   142

Index   144

To Overcome Evil with Good

Chairs scraped across the floor, spoons clattered against bowls, and the voices of a hundred men competed to be heard over the din. It was a typical day in the soup kitchen on New York City's Mott Street. Outside, a cold wind whipped along the pavement. But inside the big, noisy room, there were warmth, food, and friendly faces.

Suddenly the mood shifted. A single voice, full of rage and hatred, ripped through the room. "Shut up! Shut up or I'll kill you!"

In an instant there was a stunned silence. In the center of the room a large man with long, scraggly hair swayed drunkenly on his feet. He glared furiously around him, and the other men shrank beneath his gaze.

A tall, slender, middle-aged woman strode forward. She had been busy dishing soup into bowls, but now she saw that she was needed elsewhere. Most of the men watched her respectfully as she crossed the floor. They had known her for years. With a group of devoted helpers, she had founded this soup kitchen and shelter for the homeless where so many took refuge. Her name was Dorothy Day.

Calmly and deliberately, Dorothy approached the drunken man. "Hello," she said, smiling. "I'm very glad you've come to be with us today."

The man stared at her. His wild blue eyes seemed to bore straight through her. Dorothy sensed his madness and his rage, and she felt deeply afraid. "What are you looking at?" the man bellowed. He took a menacing step toward her.

Dorothy knew that she must be as decisive and honest as possible. "I'm looking at you," she said immediately.

"Why are you looking at me?" the man shouted.

"Because I'm standing here talking with you," she replied. "I'm Dorothy Day. What's your name?"

For a moment the man glared at her in silence. "Fred," he answered at last.

"Well, Fred," Dorothy asked, "would you like some soup?"

Fred eyed her suspiciously. "Are you going to have some?" he wanted to know.

"I'm pretty hungry," she said. "I think I will." She brought a bowl of soup for each of them, and they sat together at an empty table.

Fred watched Dorothy take a few spoonfuls, but he

didn't touch the soup she had placed before him. "Let me have *your* bowl," he growled.

"Sure," Dorothy said, sliding her bowl across to him. What was wrong, she wondered. Did he think that his own soup was poisoned?

Ravenously Fred gobbled the soup from Dorothy's bowl. Then she noticed that he was glancing at the bowl she had originally given to him. With a flash of intuition she asked, "Do you want me to have *your* soup?"

"Yes," said Fred, pushing the bowl toward her. "As a matter of fact, I do."

All the while the two of them ate, the other men in the room remained silent. There was no sound but the rattle of two spoons against two bowls and Fred's ominous muttering. His fierce, smoldering anger filled everyone with dread.

Dorothy remembered a verse from the book of Romans in the Bible. "Be not overcome with evil," it said, "but overcome evil with good." She picked up a slice of bread, broke it, and handed half to Fred. "Thank you," he said, and took a hungry bite.

"Well," Dorothy said at last, "I have to go back in the kitchen and get things ready for tomorrow's meals. I hope you'll join us again."

Fred did not answer, but somehow the tension began to ease. Here and there, voices rose again around the room. Soon the soup kitchen was as noisy as ever.

Early the next morning, one of her assistants told Dorothy that a large man with long, tangled hair wanted to see her. Fred waited at the door, greeting her with a shy smile. In his arms he carried a bulging bag of vegetables — celery, carrots, onions, and potatoes. "I thought you could use these," he said gruffly. "For the soup."

Over the years that followed, Fred became a regular guest at the soup kitchen. Dorothy Day often described their first encounter when she spoke about her life's work. In her meeting with Fred, she had managed to put the principle of Christian love into action. As the Bible counseled, she had overcome evil with good.

CHAPTER 1

A Family Apart

Throughout her long and eventful life, Dorothy Day never forgot the night of April 18, 1906 — the night of the famous San Francisco earthquake. At the time, her family was living in Oakland, California, just across the bay from San Francisco. Eight-year-old Dorothy awoke to an ominous rumble, and she lay trembling as her brass bed rolled back and forth over the polished floor. She heard terrified screams and strange sloshing sounds as water splashed from a large tank on the roof of the house.

When her bed was quiet at last, Dorothy rose to find her home a shambles. Broken dishes littered the floor. Books had tumbled from their shelves. A great, jagged crack ran up the wall of the house from the ground to the roof.

In her mind, Dorothy somehow linked the earthquake with the frightening power of God. Years later she remembered thinking of God as "a Voice, a Hand

1

stretched out to seize me, His child, and not in love." She thought that God and the earthquake were both vengeful, dangerous forces of awesome destruction. "I did not think of Jesus as God," she explains in her autobiography. "I had no one to teach me, as my parents had no one to teach them."

In San Francisco, the earthquake toppled stoves and broke gas pipes, setting off a devastating series of fires and explosions. With her brothers and sister, Dorothy gazed at the clouds of smoke that billowed across the bay. Thousands of people, left homeless by the disaster, poured into Oakland. Dorothy's mother helped the neighbors gather food and clothing for the destitute families sleeping in the park. After the terror of the earthquake, Dorothy was deeply moved by the spirit of generosity that swept over the whole community. Every family in Oakland gave what it could to help those in need. In that open-hearted sharing, Dorothy felt a spirit of love which she always remembered.

As a result of the earthquake, the newspaper office where Dorothy's father worked burned to the ground, leaving him without a job. Within a week of the calamity, the Day family boarded a train headed for Chicago.

Dorothy's father, John Day, was a sportswriter with a special interest in horseracing. He wrote for numerous papers over the years, many of them small ventures that didn't survive for long in the competitive market. Throughout Dorothy's childhood, the Day family fortunes rose and fell with the fortunes of the newspapers for which John Day worked.

The move from Oakland to Chicago uprooted Dorothy for the second time in her life. She was born in Brooklyn Heights on November 8, 1897. Soon afterward her family moved to the Brooklyn neighborhood of Bath Beach. Dorothy's earliest memories were of the sea, of running on the sand, fishing for eels, and exploring a tumbledown fisherman's shack. Throughout her life, Dorothy Day had a special love for the ocean.

Once, in search of adventure, Dorothy wandered off alone for what seemed like hours. She played happily by herself "until the sudden realization came over me that I was alone, that the world was vast and that there were evil forces therein. I can remember on the one hand my bliss — it was almost a state of natural contemplation — and then suddenly the black fear that overwhelmed me so that I ran all the way home."

The Days lived in Brooklyn until 1904, when Dorothy's father took a job that required the move to California. Now he was transplanting the family yet again, in the hope that Chicago would offer him the fresh start he needed.

At first, Chicago proved to be a cruel disappointment. John Day could not find work. The family's only income came from a few articles on racing that he managed to sell to newspapers and magazines. Dorothy, her older brothers Donald and Sam, her younger sister, Della, and their parents crowded into six dingy rooms above a saloon at 37th Street and Cottage Grove Avenue on Chicago's South Side. There John Day set to work at his typewriter, trying to write an adventure novel that he hoped would make him rich and famous.

Dorothy Day's mother, Grace Satterlee Day, was endlessly patient and resourceful. She foraged in the alleys for wooden orange crates, which she turned into bookcases. Empty nail kegs became stools around the kitchen table. And she created meals with the meager ingredients she could afford to buy. For lunch she usually served steaming bowls of potato soup. Sometimes after a long, hard day, she bathed and dressed for dinner as though she were attending a banquet. But on the table the family had nothing but bananas, bread and jelly, and tea.

Dorothy loved the nights when her mother slipped into a nostalgic mood. At such times she delighted the children with family stories that she had heard from her own parents when she was growing up in Marlboro, New York. Dorothy heard about her Great-Aunt Cassie, who used to skate down the Hudson River from Poughkeepsie to Marlboro to bake cookies at a friend's house, and then skate back home again. And there was Great-Aunt Charity's husband, a whaler, who cracked his head falling from a ship's mast and was never quite himself again. He would run into the streets in his nightshirt, and finally he drowned in a brook.

Only once in Dorothy's memory did her mother crack under the strain of their poverty. One evening, as she stood at the sink washing dishes, Grace Day suddenly burst into tears. As the children stared, horrified, she flung the plates to the floor one by one. Dorothy's brother Sam hurried the younger children into the bedroom and tried to calm them down. Later, Dorothy recalled, her father went out and bought the whole family a special treat — a big container of ice cream. His clumsy attempt at comfort only made Dorothy cry.

While his wife struggled to feed and clothe the family, John Day worked on his novel, pounding away at the typewriter until long after midnight. Because he preferred to work at night, he often slept late into the morning. He insisted that the children keep quiet, and he seldom let them bring friends to the house. Though Dorothy never felt close to her father, she knew that he wanted to protect all of them from a world that he felt was evil and dangerous. He forbade his children to read cheap thrillers and romances, stocking the bookcases with Shakespeare and Dickens instead. From an early age, Dorothy grew to love the classics of literature.

Since the Day children were relatively isolated from the world around them, they had to invent their own entertainments. Dorothy read hungrily and wrote stories and poems. She and her sister, Della, played endless games of make-believe, or sat together at the window observing the life of the busy street below. Once they spent an entire afternoon watching a man who made and sold popcorn. "We watched every motion, beginning with the popping of the corn, with the cage suspended on a wire and shaken back and forth; we watched him fill each bag and pour in a little melted butter from a white coffee pot, and shake in some salt, and we could smell it and taste it as we watched him." Though her family was reclusive, Dorothy always remembered her childhood as a happy time, and was grateful that she had so much freedom to use her imagination.

Dorothy's mother had been raised in the Episcopal Church, but Dorothy's father claimed to be an atheist. During her early childhood, Dorothy had no religious instruction of any kind. But while the family was living in California, Dorothy found a battered Bible in the attic. Out of curiosity she began reading passages aloud to her sister. She was powerfully moved by the words she read. "Slowly, . . . a new personality impressed itself upon me," she explained many years later. "I was being introduced to someone and I knew almost immediately that I was discovering God. . . . It was as though life were fuller, richer, more exciting in every way. Here was someone that I had never really known about before and yet felt to be One whom I would never forget, that I would never get away from. . . . Life would never again be the same. I had made a great discovery." Nevertheless, on the night of the earthquake, it was the frightening power of the deity that Dorothy sensed, not the endless love of the heavenly Father.

The Day children rarely attended church until they lived in Chicago. Then one day an Episcopal minister knocked on the door and urged the family to attend his church two blocks away. Donald and Sam joined the choir, and Dorothy, who was ten by that time, attended services every Sunday. She loved the Psalms and prayers, and she quickly learned many of them by heart. But church attendance was not without its worldly pleasures. Dorothy was also attracted to a young soprano soloist, a blond boy named Russell, and she gazed at him in rapture week after week.

One morning Dorothy set out to find her friend Kathryn Barrett, hoping to invite her to play outdoors. She found the door to Kathryn's apartment unlocked, and when no one answered her knock, she stepped inside. Calling her friend's name, Dorothy ran through the kitchen and the living room. Suddenly she stopped short. There, in the front bedroom, Kathryn's mother knelt on the floor praying. Mrs. Barrett turned and told Dorothy that Kathryn had gone to the store, then resumed her prayer. "I felt a burst of love toward Mrs. Barrett that I have never forgotten," Dorothy wrote more than forty years later, "a feeling of gratitude and happiness that warmed my heart."

Touched by Dorothy's interest in her Roman Catholic religion, Mrs. Barrett taught her some of the prayers that she said so faithfully every day. Dorothy was enthralled. Night after night she knelt by her bed, praying until her knees ached and she shivered with cold. Della, who shared her room, begged her to climb into bed and tell her a story. Dorothy, in turn, urged Della to get out of bed and join her in prayer. "So we began to practice being saints," Dorothy wrote later. "It was a game with us."

Dorothy had no way of knowing how much her religious feelings would change as she grew older. But when she was a child, religion was a fascinating game, an enchanting make-believe, one more piece of the puzzle called growing up.

Fortunately, the Day family's brush with poverty was soon over. When Dorothy was twelve, her father obtained a job with a Chicago paper called the *Inter Ocean*. As soon as he had a steady income, the Days moved to pleasanter quarters on the city's North Side. Dorothy had especially fond memories of a warm, spacious house they rented on Webster Avenue near Lincoln Park, a home that afforded plenty of privacy for everyone.

The Webster Avenue house had a library, a book-lined room with a fireplace and a large, round table surrounded by easy chairs. Sometimes Dorothy worked at a little desk in the corner while her mother sewed. At other times she read, seated at the table with her brothers and sister, munching apples or sipping hot chocolate before bedtime. "To draw the curtains at night on a street where people bent against the wind, . . . and to turn to a room where a fire glowed in the basket grate and a smell of fresh bread filled the house," she wrote in her autobiography entitled *The Long Loneliness*, "this was comfort, security, peace, community."

When Dorothy was fourteen, the last of the Day children was born — her baby brother, John. Grace Day was ill and depressed for months after the baby's birth, and much of his care became Dorothy's responsibility. Often at night, when John was fussy and refused to fall asleep, she would rock him until her back and shoulders ached. At four in the morning he would awaken again, and their mother would carry him to a small crib set up in Dorothy's room. Soon John would wake Dorothy by bouncing on his springy mattress and cooing to the birds and milk wagons he heard outside. By four-thirty she would have to get up, go down to the kitchen, and heat his bottle.

The more the baby demanded from her, the more intensely Dorothy loved him. The Days were not an affectionate family, and in most situations Dorothy was painfully uncomfortable with kisses and embraces. Yet she could lavish affection on her baby brother. He helped to fill a deep need in her that she had scarcely known existed before.

At about the same time that John was born, Dorothy experienced love of a different kind. She developed a passionate crush on Armin Hand, a young man who lived down the street. He was married and the father of two small children, and he and Dorothy never exchanged a word. Yet they passed each other several times a day as Dorothy pushed John up and down the block in his carriage. Dorothy "hungered for his look," she wrote later, and Armin never failed to turn toward her with an expression that told her he knew there was something special between them.

Armin Hand was a violinist, and during the summer he conducted band concerts in Lincoln Park on Sunday and Wednesday evenings. Dorothy and her sister, Della, attended his concerts without fail. Dorothy thrilled to every moment. She loved the walk to the park, especially after a rain, when tiny toads appeared on the path like darting jewels. She loved to sit in the stands, reveling in the music and gazing at Armin Hand. Then there was the walk home again, talking over the delights of the evening with Della, or losing herself in quiet contemplation.

Like most teenagers, Dorothy was absorbed in her exploration of human love. But she felt a profound longing for spiritual love as well. This spiritual need can be glimpsed in a letter that she wrote to her friend Henrietta when she was fifteen:

We went to the park Friday, and Della and I went on the merry-go-round and the lake boat. We each had fifty cents and it was with regret that I saw the money go. It seemed a shameless waste, but then I realized there was more for God's children and it will come to them when they need it. . . .

Yesterday I took the baby to the park. He was sweet and good, and the sky was a dark, deep blue, all flecked with purplish clouds. The trees were rustling and the sun flickered on my book. I was happy but not in the right way. I did not have the spiritual happiness that I crave, only a wicked thrilling feeling at my heart. . . .

Della and I have been following an exciting serial in the movies and father lets us go only on Sunday afternoons when it's rainy, but never at any other time during the week. My ideas have changed about Sunday. I have learned that it is rather hypocritical to be so strict on Sunday and not on every other day of the week. Every day belongs to God and every day we are to serve Him doing His pleasure. And "as every good gift is prepared for them that love God," and moving pictures are a good thing, if you stop to think of the educational advantages of them, therefore, I can see nothing wrong in going to a show and pleasing Della and incidentally myself. . . .

It is wrong to think so much about human love. All those feelings and cravings that come to us are sexual desires. We are prone to have them at this age, I suppose, but I think they are impure. It is sensual and God is spiritual. We must harden ourselves to these feelings, for God is love and God is all, so the only love is of God and is spiritual without taint of earthliness. I am afraid I have never really experienced this love or I would never crave the sensual love or the thrill that comes with the meeting of lips.

I know it seems foolish to try to be so Christlike — but God says we can — why else His command, "Be ye therefore perfect."

11

Oh, surely it is a continual strife and my spirit is weary.

Looking back on this letter many years later, Dorothy felt that it was "filled with pomp and vanity and piety." Yet it reveals a young girl of unusual sensitivity, searching for a happiness that she knew could not come from worldly things.

Dorothy was an excellent student, and she thoroughly enjoyed her studies. She loved languages and worked hard at her Latin. One of her high-school teachers, a Mr. Matheson, taught Greek to Dorothy and a select group of her classmates on his own time after school.

As Dorothy began her final year of high school, her older brother Donald took a job with a small paper called the *Day Book*. The *Day Book* (the name had nothing to do with the Day family) sympathized strongly with the rising labor movement and covered the struggles of working men and women in Chicago. After studying the papers that Donald brought home, Dorothy began to read the work of Carl Sandburg, Upton Sinclair, and Jack London, writers who called the nation's attention to the injustices of the class system in the industrial world. The labor leader Eugene Debs became Dorothy's hero.

As the autumn days grew shorter, Dorothy turned away from Lincoln Park and set off to explore the grim streets of Chicago's West Side. Pushing John's carriage for miles, she passed noisy taverns, whirring factories, and basement apartments whose grilled windows peered out at the level of the sidewalk. Even in the drabbest surroundings, Dorothy found that people planted gardens of flowers and vegetables. She admired the marigolds, geraniums, and tomatoes that brightened the dreary landscape. She realized that even the poorest people yearned for beauty.

Dorothy knew that Christ had rejected "the things of the world," but she was certain that God did not intend human beings to live in dire poverty. Why, she asked herself, were most of the Christians she knew so complacent, when there was so much suffering all around them? Often she thought of the aftermath of the San Francisco earthquake, when she had experienced such a sense of community, of sharing. She saw that spirit of open-handed giving as an ideal toward which all people might strive. "I did not want just the few, the missionary-minded people like the Salvation Army, to be kind to the poor," she wrote later. "I wanted everyone to be kind. I wanted every home to be open to the lame, the halt and the blind. . . . Only then did people really live, love their brothers. In such love was the abundant life and I did not have the slightest idea how to find it."

That year the *Inter Ocean* ceased publication, and once more Dorothy's father was out of work. Dorothy feared that she would never realize her dream of attending college. But to her joy her knowledge of Greek and Latin helped her win a scholarship to the University of

Illinois in Urbana. The scholarship provided only three hundred dollars a year, and Dorothy would have to earn money for her books and meals. But such details did not worry her as she boarded the train that would carry her into this new adventure. "I was happy as a lark at leaving home," she recalled in her autobiography. "I was sixteen and filled with a sense of great independence. I was on my own, and no longer to be cared for by the family."

It hardly mattered what courses she studied. She wanted experience. She wanted to reach beyond her books and discover the real world for herself.

CHAPTER 2

To Change the World

Dorothy Day entered the University of Illinois in the fall of 1914. At first she was delighted by her new sense of freedom. She came and went as she pleased, often staying out late at night. She only attended the classes that interested her, and she spent luxurious hours reading books of her own choosing. She was already a devoted reader of Upton Sinclair and Jack London; now she discovered a love for the great Russian novelists Tolstoy, Dostoyevski, and Gorky. Her passion for these Russian writers remained with her for the rest of her life.

After a few months, however, the novelty of independence wore off, and Dorothy became intensely homesick. Sometimes she cried herself to sleep at night and awoke crying in the morning. She missed her baby brother John with a deep, constant ache. He was two years old now, lively and responsive, and she knew that he was growing up without her. "He loved me dearly," she wrote in her autobiography. "I had been a mother to him, so that he clung to me and was bone of my bone and flesh of my flesh. I had never loved anyone or anything as I loved him, with a love that was open and unreserved, entailing hardship but bringing also peace and joy."

Despite her misery, Dorothy never considered leaving college. She felt that the loss of closeness to her brother was inevitable, a simple fact of life. Somehow she must live through it and move on.

Dorothy's concern for the poor and downtrodden continued to build. In her determination to help the struggling masses of humanity, she began to put her religious feelings behind her. The churches were doing little to fight social injustice. But the Socialist Party promised that it would change the world. Dorothy thrilled with excitement whenever she heard the Communist slogan, "Workers of the world, unite! You have nothing to lose but your chains!"

One day during class, a professor whom Dorothy greatly admired brought up the subject of religion. He remarked that religion had comforted people for centuries; for that reason, it should not be criticized. But to Dorothy his statement meant that religion was a sort of crutch which should not be necessary for people who were truly strong.

Ever since that long-ago afternoon when she had found the Bible in the attic, religious faith had been a guiding force in Dorothy's life. She had known a deep yearning toward and trust in God. Now she concluded that she should not, and did not, need a god any longer.

(Many years later, when she wrote about her experiences, Dorothy Day worried that her years without faith might set a bad example for others. She feared that young people who learned her life story might say to themselves, "Dorothy Day lived a free and easy life, so why shouldn't I?" She never ceased to regret the mistakes she made in her youth, and she hoped that others could avoid the same pitfalls.)

Haunted by her professor's words, Dorothy stopped attending church services. Deliberately, systematically, she took up smoking and swearing. She thought of religion as an addictive drug that she wanted to cleanse from her system. She looked with contempt upon pious fellow students. Young people shouldn't be at peace in such a troubled world, she decided. Youth ought to be at war.

Money was always in short supply during Dorothy's first year at college. Often she went hungry because she spent her meager funds on books. For several months she boarded with a poverty-stricken professor, his wife, and their five children. She paid her way by washing the family's laundry, bending over a scrub board until her back ached and her hands were sore and raw. When winter came, the arctic winds whipped across the prairie and whistled through the cracks in the old house. Dorothy's bare room had no carpets and was icy cold. When she came home in the evenings, she scrambled into bed, but even bundled under the blankets she couldn't keep warm.

During her first semester on campus, Dorothy came and went alone, a tall, sturdily built girl with thick dark hair and beautiful almond-shaped eyes. She made no close friends but kept to herself, lost in her books and her homesickness. During her second semester, however, Dorothy joined a literary club called the Scribblers. Several of the club members were impressed by the first story she showed them, a description of three days she spent with nothing to eat except salted peanuts.

One of the other Scribblers was Rayna Simons, a girl from Chicago who lived in a special residence for Jewish students. Dorothy had long admired Rayna from a distance, struck by her warmth, her intensity, and her flaming crown of curly red hair. The two girls quickly formed a deep and lasting friendship. The following year they roomed together, and Rayna generously helped Dorothy through many lean times when her money ran low.

Dorothy, Rayna, and Rayna's fiancé, Raph (Samson Raphaelson), became a happy threesome. They attended plays, concerts, and lectures, criticized each other's stories, and went to the country for wonderful all-day picnics. Dorothy sensed that this friendship was rare and unique, and she tried to treasure every moment.

But even in these idyllic days, Dorothy never forgot that the poor and oppressed were all around her. While she had the luxury of attending college, she knew that thousands of girls her age worked long, grueling hours on factory assembly lines. She joined the Socialist Party and attended several meetings, but she found them long and boring. The local newspaper, which liked much of her writing, refused to print articles she wrote that condemned the existing class structure.

Why, Dorothy asked herself, were people always eager to solve social problems but reluctant to prevent those problems from developing in the first place? There were nurseries to care for children whose mothers worked in factories; why couldn't the fathers be paid more, so that the mothers wouldn't have to work? Doctors tended men and women with tuberculosis and other diseases brought about by unhealthy living conditions; why were those conditions allowed to persist? Unable to find a way to make a difference in the world, Dorothy often felt frustrated and restless.

Dorothy's second year in Urbana flew past. In her autobiography she described her glorious days with Rayna and Raph through the changing seasons: "The burning heat of the prairies, the dry cold of the winter snows, the smell of the upturned blue-black earth in spring. We enjoyed it all because of Rayna, who gave her loving heart to both of us, entering into all our plans and dreams and making us feel capable of great things."

Dorothy's time at the University of Illinois was soon at an end. In the spring of 1916, her father took a job with the *Morning Telegraph,* a leading paper in New York

City, and the Days left Chicago forever. Dorothy considered herself quite independent by this time, but she couldn't bear the thought of staying in Urbana while her family was so far away. Although she knew that she would miss Rayna terribly, she decided to leave school and look for work on a newspaper in New York. After completing two years of college, she plunged into her life's next great adventure.

Living at home was not easy for Dorothy after two years of independence. She had gone off to college a shy, awkward girl of sixteen. She returned a young woman, bursting with new ideas that her parents couldn't understand. Immediately she ran into conflict with her father, who felt that women didn't belong in newspaper work. When Dorothy announced that she was looking for a job with one of the New York papers, her father contacted all of the editors he knew and told them not to hire her.

Through the long, hot summer of 1916, Dorothy tramped the streets of New York in search of work. Sometimes she went exploring, riding the subways, crossing bridges, watching people in the parks. The poverty she saw in New York seemed deeper, more entrenched, more demoralizing than anything she had witnessed in the Midwest. "The very odors were different," she wrote years later. "The sight of homeless and workless men lounging on street corners or sleeping in doorways in broad sunlight appalled me. The sight of cheap lodging houses, dingy restaurants, the noise of subways and elevated railways, the clanging of streetcars jarred my senses. Above all the smell from the tenements, coming up from basements and areaways, from dank halls, horrified me. It is a smell like no other in the world and one never can become accustomed to it. . . . There is a smell in the walls of such tenements, a damp ooze coming from them in the halls. One's very clothes smell of it. It is not the smell of life, but the smell of the grave."

As she walked the streets, or sat at home in the midst of her family, Dorothy felt a sense of overwhelming loneliness. "In all that great city of seven millions, I found no friends; I had no work; I was separated from my fellows. Silence in the midst of city noises oppressed me. My own silence, the feeling that I had no one to talk to, overwhelmed me so that my very throat was constricted; my heart was heavy with unuttered thoughts; I wanted to weep my loneliness away." Somehow, Dorothy felt that this terrible isolation could be relieved only if she lived among the poor people she saw around her.

In the fall of 1916, Dorothy finally landed a job at a struggling Socialist daily, the New York *Call*. On a salary of five dollars a week, she rented a room with a Jewish family in a tenement on the city's Lower East Side. In one of her first articles she described the rigors of life on her low income. Humorously she entitled it "New York *Call's* Diet Squad Tries Life on Five Dollars a Weak."

21

The friends Dorothy made at the *Call* more than offset the hardships. Often after work, which she might finish as late as three A.M., Dorothy joined a crowd of reporters, artists, and political radicals at a restaurant in Greenwich Village. Over heaping plates of pancakes they argued and laughed, told stories, and made glorious plans. One of her closest friends was Mike Gold, a writer and editor who shared many of her ideas about changing the social order. Another was a hard-drinking young artist named Peggy Baird. Although enormous changes lay ahead for her, Dorothy kept her friendships with Mike and Peggy alive throughout her lifetime.

The threat of war hung over all of Dorothy's late-night discussions. All of Europe had been engulfed in warfare since 1914. Now the United States was preparing to enter the conflict, which is remembered today as World War I. Sometimes at night Dorothy pitched in when antiwar activists pasted posters to walls and display windows. For several weeks she worked with the Anti-Conscription League, protesting the military draft.

In the spring of 1917, Dorothy began to work for *The Masses,* a Socialist paper edited by the writer Max Eastman. *The Masses* was slightly more substantial than the *Call,* and Dorothy's salary doubled — reaching the princely sum of ten dollars a week. Floyd Dell, one of the editors at the paper, later described Dorothy as "an awkward young enthusiast with beautiful slanting eyes." Dell taught Dorothy everything he knew about putting a newspaper together. During the summer, he rented a cottage at the seashore and tried to write a novel, leaving Dorothy in sole charge of *The Masses*.

That summer was a joyous time for Dorothy. She moved into an apartment in Greenwich Village and held a constant open house. Her old friend Rayna came from Chicago to join her, and the two young women hosted one dinner party after another. Twelve people could sit around their dining-room table. Sometimes Dorothy and Rayna met homeless people in the park and invited them in for the night. They would give up their own beds for their guests and sit up all night talking in the kitchen. Once a group of men from the park stayed up all night arguing about the draft. To Dorothy's dismay, after all of their debating, every one of them signed up to go to war the next morning.

Like so many of the papers where Dorothy's father worked, *The Masses* didn't survive for long. In December 1917, it printed its final issue. Dorothy was once again looking for a job.

The war in Europe was not the only concern of radical social reformers in 1917. The long struggle to gain women the right to vote was also gathering momentum. In November, a few weeks before *The Masses* stopped publication, Dorothy piled onto a bus with her friend Peggy Baird and a group of other women and headed for Washington, D.C. In the nation's capital they launched a series of protest demonstrations for women's suffrage.

23

Carrying banners and placards, the women marched toward the White House. Squads of policemen flanked the demonstrators, and crowds of spectators pressed close to watch the excitement. Angry men shouted that the president had more important things to think about, that the women were unpatriotic troublemakers. When a sailor tried to wrench Dorothy's banner out of her hands, a scuffle ensued. The police moved in and arrested thirty-five demonstrators. The women were tried the next morning and found guilty, but the judge postponed their sentence.

When the women picketed again that afternoon, the same procedure was repeated. But when they picketed once again and were arrested, they refused to post bail, so they were kept in the House of Detention. The next morning, Dorothy and most of the others were sentenced to spend thirty days in jail. They were loaded into prison vans, then driven to a train station and put onto a train bound for an unknown destination. As they chugged through the countryside, rumors flew among the women. Again and again one name was repeated: Occoquan.

Dorothy and the other demonstrators were indeed bound for Occoquan, an infamous workhouse for female prisoners located in northern Virginia. As soon as they arrived, they were marched to the administration building for processing. A matron demanded their names, but by agreement they all refused to answer.

The women had decided among themselves that

they must demand to be treated as political prisoners, since they were protesting for a legitimate political cause. Under international conventions, political prisoners were granted certain rights denied to ordinary convicts. They were permitted to wear their own clothes rather than prison uniforms; they could receive mail and visitors; they could purchase extra food if they wished; and they were entitled to legal council. The women decided that if their demands were not met, they would stage a ten-day hunger strike.

The spokeswoman of the group asked to see the prison superintendent. She came from a wealthy Philadelphia family and so was used to wielding power and influence. Eventually the superintendent appeared. He was a big, gruff man named Whittaker, notorious for his cruelty toward the prisoners in his charge. As soon as the woman from Philadelphia began to explain the group's demands, Whittaker gestured toward the door of the office. A squadron of guards burst into the room. Outnumbering the women two to one, the guards seized them brutally and half-carried, half-dragged them to the cell block.

Terrified, Dorothy fought to free herself and reach Peggy. In the tumult she was slammed hard against an iron bench, then thrown to the ground. Ironically, the *New York Times* later reported on the incident as "a prison riot."

Dorothy was locked into a cell with Lucy Byrnes, a schoolteacher from Brooklyn. For several hours, Lucy was handcuffed to the cell bars so that she couldn't sit down. But the first morning after the lockup, Lucy was taken to another cell, and Dorothy was alone. The women had no privacy, even when they used the toilet. But worst of all were the hunger and the grinding monotony. All day Dorothy lay on the thin straw mattress, trying to sleep to pass the time, while pain gnawed at her empty stomach. Three times a day the guards brought warm milk and fragrant fresh toast, and three times a day Dorothy refused the food until it was taken away again.

As the days passed, Dorothy lost sight of the cause that had brought her to prison. She thought only of her fellow prisoners, suffering hunger, deprivation, and loneliness in cells all over the world. She marveled that human beings could treat one another so callously. "I had an ugly sense of the futility of human effort, man's helpless misery, the triumph of might," she wrote later. "Man's dignity was but a word and a lie. Evil triumphed. I was a petty creature, filled with self-deception, self-importance, unreal, false, and so, rightly scorned and punished. I was willing not only to say two and two were five, but to think it."

On her second day at Occoquan, Dorothy asked the guards to bring her a Bible. Two days later, her request was granted. In the dim light of her cell, Dorothy read the Psalms over and over. Later she recalled, "All through those weary first days in jail . . . the only thoughts that brought comfort to my soul were those lines in the Psalms that expressed the terror and misery of man suddenly stricken and abandoned. Solitude and hunger and weariness of spirit — these sharpened my perceptions so that I suffered not only my own sorrow but the sorrows of those around me. I was no longer myself. I was man. I was no longer a young girl, part of a radical movement seeking justice for the oppressed. I was the oppressed." That sense of oneness with all suffering humanity brought her both pain and a deep consolation. Yet even then, she was dismayed by her feelings. She still tried to assure herself that she didn't really need religion. She was only reading the Bible as a piece of literature.

After six days, the fasting suffragists were transferred to the prison's hospital wing. Here the cells were brighter and warmer. Peggy was next door to Dorothy. Peggy had somehow managed to keep a pencil stub, and the two young women exchanged notes they wrote on toilet paper, sliding them beneath the radiator that separated their cells. For two more days, they both kept to the hunger strike. But on the eighth day, Peggy gave in and ate a slice of toast. She urged Dorothy to do the same, and slipped a piece of crust into her cell. Slowly, crumb by crumb, Dorothy savored the first food she had tasted in more than a week. She could not recall an experience richer or more sensual — and she didn't feel guilty. "I continued the protest we had undertaken," she commented later. "Cheating the prison authorities was quite in order, I reasoned."

At last, on the tenth day of their imprisonment, the suffragists were informed that their demands would be met. They were given back their clothes, they received their mail, and they were allowed to walk the corridors. Having won the battle, the women ended their hunger strike. At first they were given mild foods such as milk, toast, and broth. But soon the prison hospital prepared delicious meals beyond their wildest imagining. Within a few days they had all regained their strength and were ready to be moved to the city jail in Washington.

At the city jail, the suffragists were granted the same relative freedom. They were allowed to choose their own cells, and they had the run of the corridors from eight in the morning until eight at night. Dorothy read, chatted with friends, wrote letters, and observed the ups and downs of daily prison life with her keen reporter's eye.

Now the degradation of Occoquan seemed far away and almost unreal. Dorothy felt ashamed that she had turned to the Psalms for comfort. She had simply been at a low point, she told herself, weakened by hunger and despair. Now that she was strong once more, she would cast aside the crutch of religion forever.

CHAPTER 3

Adrift

When she returned to New York after her jail term in Washington, Dorothy Day wrote articles for several Socialist newspapers. She earned barely enough money to survive, and she lived in a series of bleak furnished rooms. The country was at war, and everywhere austerity measures were in force. Citizens were exhorted to spend "heatless Mondays" and "meatless Tuesdays" in order to conserve resources for the war effort.

As always, friendships enriched Dorothy's life. She spent most of her spare time with the Provincetown Players, a group of playwrights and actors who had recently moved to Manhattan from Cape Cod. The leading member of the group was a talented young dramatist named Eugene O'Neill. Late into the night Dorothy and O'Neill would sit deep in conversation over drinks in the back room of a Greenwich Village tavern that was nicknamed Hell Hole. They would sing old songs and discuss art, literature, and life. O'Neill was often bitter and depressed. Sometimes, when he would drink too much, Dorothy would walk him home and tuck him into bed for the night.

Eugene O'Neill loved poetry. Dorothy always remembered the night he recited "The Hound of Heaven," a long religious work by the nineteenth-century British poet Francis Thompson:

I fled Him, down the nights and down the days;
I fled Him, down the arches of the years;
I fled Him, down the labyrinthine ways
Of my own mind; and in the mist of tears
I hid from Him, and under running laughter.

Dorothy was haunted by the words. They drew her back to an earlier time, when religion had played such an important part in her life. She knew that she herself was fleeing from God, that he pursued her like the heavenly hound in the poem, and that someday they would meet at last. Years later, she reflected, "Since he brought me such a consciousness of God, since he recited to me 'The Hound of Heaven' I owe him [O'Neill] my prayers."

By the spring, Dorothy had grown restless. She felt that she was drifting, that her life lacked any real purpose. She was doing nothing to change the social order or to help individuals who struggled and suffered. When a close friend died from a drug overdose, she determined to make a major change. She enrolled in a nurses' training program at King's County Hospital in Brooklyn.

Since the United States had entered the war in Europe, many qualified nurses had gone overseas with the Red Cross to care for wounded soldiers. As a consequence, American hospitals faced a serious nursing shortage. Dorothy and most of her friends deplored the war as the devastating result of imperialism and capitalism. By working as a nurse, Dorothy worried that she might be indirectly aiding the war effort, freeing more nurses to tend the troops. Yet she felt that desperately ill people were in need of care on the homefront. By becoming a nurse she could do something very real to help them.

Dorothy and her sister, Della, joined the training program in April of 1918. Their mother was delighted; she hoped that Dorothy would finally settle down. From the first, the work was pitilessly hard. The novice nurses toiled from seven A.M. until seven P.M. They attended classes for two hours in the afternoon, but they spent most of their time caring for patients on the ward. They changed bedding, bathed patients, emptied bedpans, and doled out medications. Always they tried to make their patients as comfortable as possible. Dorothy was impressed with the compassion shown by the hospital staff. "My experience there reassured me as to the care one received from the city," Dorothy wrote later. "It was a care given to citizens, not to paupers. And it was all free."

Dorothy's first patient was a ninety-four-year-old

woman, shriveled by age and nearly bald. She shrieked and struggled when Dorothy tried to give her a bath. She didn't want a bath, she screamed — what she wanted was her wig, which had been taken by the hospital authorities. Another nurse spoke to her soothingly, but the woman continued to rant. At last a more experienced nurse brought the patient a hat to cover her bare head, and she finally grew calm. Dorothy recognized that the woman needed more than hygiene, even more than words of kindness. She needed to be respected as a person of dignity.

After spending several months on the fractures ward, chiefly caring for elderly patients with broken hips, Dorothy was transferred to a ward where all the patients were suffering from influenza. At that time, an influenza epidemic was sweeping the world. Penicillin and other antibiotics had not yet been developed, and millions of people died. At the end of her shift, Dorothy would help wrap the dead in sheets and carry their bodies from the ward. In the morning when she came on duty, she saw the departing night nurses wrapping the bodies of the men who had died while she slept.

"Nursing was like newspaper work," Dorothy wrote in her autobiography. "It was impossible to suffer long over the tragedies which took place every day. One was too close to them to have perspective. They happened too continuously. They weighed on you, gave you a still and subdued feeling, but the very fact that you were continually busy left you no time to brood."

Sometimes the hospital offered glimpses of beauty that buoyed Dorothy over the harshest moments. On mild days, she wandered the gardens on the hospital grounds. She watched squirrels, sparrows, and pigeons, and visited with the patients who were well enough to sit outdoors. In the midst of tragedy, with the ugliness of pain and deprivation all around her, she felt renewed by the peace of nature.

"There was another beauty which came into my life at that time," she wrote later. "Every Sunday morning Miss Adams [another young nurse] went to early Mass [at the chapel on the hospital grounds] and I dragged myself out of my heavy sleep and went with her." Gently, quietly, Dorothy found herself drawn once again toward the faith that had meant so much to her years before. Like her long-ago mentor Mrs. Barrett, Miss Adams was a Roman Catholic. Dorothy found beauty in the pageant of the Mass and in the devotion of the simple men and women who went to worship.

Those early-morning services reawakened her old longings and brought to mind questions she had not yet been able to answer:

> One day, I told myself as I knelt there, I would have to stop and think, to question my own position: "What is man, that Thou art mindful of him, O Lord?" What were we here for, what were we doing, what was the meaning of our lives?
>
> One thing I was sure of, and that was that these

33

fellow workers and I were performing an act of worship. I felt that it was necessary for man to worship, that he was most truly himself when engaged in that act.

Dorothy seemed to be in the process of finding her spiritual center, but emotionally she was still on a kind of roller coaster. Soon after her arrival at King's County, Dorothy met Lionel Moise, an orderly in the hospital kitchen. Moise was a strange, intense man, a hard-drinking brawler with a battered face. From their first encounter Dorothy found herself hopelessly in love with him. His life was a series of adventures and contradictions. He had been born in Kansas to French-Jewish parents. He had worked as a reporter on newspapers across the United States. He had served as cameraman with a movie-making crew in the jungles of Venezuela. Now he drifted from job to job, awaiting his big break.

Every morning Dorothy would stop by the kitchen and Moise would prepare her breakfast. She also found excuses to drop by at odd moments to steal a swift embrace. But Moise was careful never to promise that they would have a future together. He had no interest in family ties.

One day Moise announced that he had found work acting in a play and would be leaving the hospital. Dorothy was devastated and begged to be able to see him again. Reluctantly he gave her his address and, after further hesitation, he invited her to move in with him.

In 1918 it was considered socially unacceptable for a man and a woman to live together without being married. But Dorothy didn't care about social conventions. She wanted only to be with Lionel Moise.

Fearfully, Dorothy confided her plans to her mother. But Grace Day took the news surprisingly well. Two weeks after Dorothy moved into Moise's apartment, her mother sent them a "wedding present" of flatware for six.

Dorothy threw herself into the role of homemaker. She enjoyed shopping, cooking, sewing, and keeping the apartment neat and clean. But Moise was not an easy man to live with. Sometimes he became enraged with jealousy, and their time together churned with fights and accusations.

In January of 1919, two months after the war was over, Dorothy went to her supervisor at King's County and explained that she had decided to leave nursing. She was exhausted by the long hours, and she felt that journalism was really her true vocation. Angrily the supervisor told Dorothy that she had always considered herself too good for the work she had been doing, and she taunted Dorothy about her ambition to write. Dorothy felt that she had been a good and sympathetic nurse, and that she was making the only decision she could. Her supervisor's ridicule hurt her deeply.

Within months, Dorothy faced an even more bitter blow. She discovered that she was pregnant. When Moise found out, he told her that he would leave her.

Desperate to win him back, Dorothy underwent an abortion in the sordid back room of an East Side apartment. She returned home only to find that Moise had packed his belongings and left town. His farewell note did not tell her where he had gone, but stated that there was no hope for reconciliation between them.

Her tragic love affair with Moise left Dorothy deeply shaken. She was haunted by the fact that she had aborted their unborn child. She looked upon her abortion and the desperate passion that led up to it as a grievous wrong. It remained with her as an indelible stain that forever seemed to mar her life. Even in old age, she could not bring herself to speak of the experience to her closest friends.

Dorothy sought escape from her grief by flinging herself into a new and very different relationship. In the spring of 1920, at the age of twenty-two, she married Barkley Tobey, a forty-two-year-old business promoter. Together they set off on a leisurely tour of Europe. Dorothy wandered the streets of London, remembering her favorite novels by Charles Dickens. In Paris she relived scenes from Balzac, de Maupassant, and other French writers. She loved Italy best of all — the smell of olive oil, the clamor of church bells, the warm laughter of the Italian people.

But Dorothy's marriage was short-lived. She and Tobey were ill-suited to each other from the start, and they separated in less than a year. In a letter to a friend, Dorothy explained, "I felt I had used him and was ashamed." In fact, she was so ashamed of this entire chapter in her life that she made no reference to her marriage or to her relationship with Lionel Moise in *The Long Loneliness*. Instead she explained that she had little to say about the next few years after she left nursing, and added, "I have never intended to write an autobiography. I have always wanted instead to tell of things that brought me to God and reminded me of God."

For six months after she and her husband parted, Dorothy lived on the idyllic Italian island of Capri. There she devoted her time to writing. When she finally returned to the United States, she carried with her the manuscript of a novel entitled *The Eleventh Virgin*. The story of a young woman's quest for meaning, it closely paralleled the events of Dorothy's own life.

Dorothy still cherished the hope that she could be reunited with Lionel Moise, that somehow they might have a life together. By now Moise was working on a newspaper in Chicago. When she learned of his whereabouts, Dorothy rushed off to find him. For a short time they were together again, but their relationship was as turbulent as ever. Finally Moise left her once more, for the last time. Meanwhile, Dorothy drifted from one job to another, working as an artist's model, a library helper, a restaurant cashier, and a newspaper reporter.

Soon after arriving in Chicago, Dorothy had met Mae Kramer, a former drug addict who had spent years in and out of prison. Though their backgrounds were very different, Dorothy and Mae shared a common bond —

Mae, too, was in love with Lionel Moise. One evening Dorothy received a desperate phone call from Mae, who was spending the night at a flophouse (a cheap rooming house) run by the International Workers of the World (IWW). Would Dorothy please bring her some food and extra clothes? She was frightened and lonely and needed help.

The IWW, known also as the Wobblies, was a Communist-backed labor organization. In Chicago, the IWW published a Communist newspaper and operated a flophouse for indigent men. The group also organized labor strikes and rallies. Because of its activities and its affiliation with the Communist Party, the IWW was constantly under police surveillance. On the night when Dorothy went to visit her friend Mae, the police decided to raid the IWW flophouse.

Near midnight, Dorothy and Mae heard heavy footsteps on the stairs. Fists pounded on the door of their room. Two leering police detectives declared that the women were under arrest and hurried them down to the street. For more than an hour they waited in the cold, along with several of the IWW men, for a patrol wagon to take them to the police station. As people passed by, staring and gawking, Dorothy felt utterly humiliated.

At the police station, Dorothy and Mae were charged with residing at a "disorderly house." In other words, they were both accused of prostitution. And for the second time in her life, Dorothy Day found herself locked in a jail cell.

When Dorothy had been with the suffragists in Washington, she had felt a sense of pride in fighting for a just cause. But in this circumstance she knew only shame, terror, and total degradation. None of her friends knew where she was. No one at the police station or the jail believed in her innocence. She was assumed to be guilty, even before the scheduled trial, and she had no chance to make even a single phone call. She was being treated like a common criminal, a woman of the streets.

For the next two days, Dorothy and Mae shared a cell with more than a dozen other accused prostitutes. Mae and the other women were all thoroughly used to life behind bars. They joked with the guards, sang loud, raucous songs, and played endless card games to pass the long hours. But Dorothy huddled on her filthy bunk, miserable and alone. The other women tried to comfort her, assuring her that she would soon get over her fears. But no gesture of kindness, nothing anyone could say eased her wretchedness.

On the morning that the women were being taken into court, Dorothy happened to see a friend of hers, Manny Gomez, on the street outside the courthouse. He ran over to talk with her and, when he realized the predicament she was in, promised to contact her friends and a lawyer. Dorothy was greatly relieved, but she and Mae still wound up being taken to the city jail that day, since they were unable to pay their bail.

Dorothy and Mae remained in jail for only a few days, but it was an experience that stayed with Dorothy for a lifetime. The two women were stripped, searched, given prison clothes, and locked in cells. In the cell next door, a woman addicted to drugs suffered the agony of withdrawal. She beat her head against the bars and howled in agony. "I have never heard such anguish, such unspeakable suffering," Dorothy wrote in her autobiography. "No woman in childbirth, no cancer patient, no one in the long year I had spent in King's County Hospital had revealed suffering like this. I pressed my hands to my ears, and covered my head with my pillow to try to muffle the sounds. It was most harrowing to think that this pain, this torture, was in a way self-inflicted, with full knowledge of the torture involved. The madness, the perverseness of this seeking for pleasure that was bound to be accompanied by such mortal agony was hard to understand. To see human beings racked, by their own will, made one feel the depth of the disorder of the world." When Dorothy had been at Occoquan, she had felt closer to God, but this experience was different: "I just suffered desperately and desired to be freed from my suffering, with a most urgent and selfish passion. The instinct for self-preservation made me forget everything but a frantic desire for freedom."

Dorothy gained her freedom within just a few days, after Manny Gomez obtained a lawyer. The charges against her were dismissed, and both she and Mae were released. Once again, Dorothy realized, her good luck and fortunate connections had saved her. But thousands of less privileged men and women languished without hope behind bars.

Shattered by her prison experience and by the permanent loss of Lionel Moise, Dorothy endured a long, hard winter. She had a job with the City News Bureau, but she was sick off and on. Her only comfort was the friendship she developed with two Catholic girls, Blanche and Bee, both of whom confided in her freely. Their reliance on prayer to help them through difficult times reminded Dorothy of her old friend Mrs. Barrett, who had taught her about Catholicism when she was a child. Dorothy envied her friends the solace of their faith. She herself was still very far from the religious belief that had been part of her childhood, and she felt lost and alone. Nevertheless, some of the reading she did that winter made her feel that she "could be at home in the Catholic Church, without becoming a Catholic."

During the fall of 1923, Dorothy was tired of the way things were going in Chicago. Among other things, her manuscript had been accepted by a publisher, but she still didn't know how much money she would make from it. She decided she needed a change, so she and a friend named Mary set out on a new adventure together. They boarded a train and headed for New Orleans, Louisiana, where they hoped to find work.

With her journalism background, Dorothy quickly found a job with the *New Orleans Item,* the city's largest daily paper. Her first assignment was a feature story on taxi dancers, young women who worked in bars and dance halls, where customers paid to dance with them. By working for several nights as a taxi dancer herself, Dorothy wrote a shocking exposé, revealing a world of corruption and illegal drugs.

Dorothy loved New Orleans, with its flowers, its stately homes, and its beautiful old churches. She and her friend Mary rented a bright, spacious room with a balcony, near the cathedral on Jackson Square, and they lived on shrimp, rice, and rabbit stew.

Often when her work for the paper was done, Dorothy stopped at the cathedral on the square. She loved to observe the ancient rituals performed there, although she didn't understand all of their sacred meaning. Seeing Dorothy's fascination with Catholicism, her friend Mary gave her a rosary. It was the first rosary Dorothy had ever owned, and she kept it with her for many years.

In April of 1924, *The Eleventh Virgin* was published by Charles and Albert Boni. The reviews were mixed; the *New York Times* called it "one more adolescent novel." In later years, Dorothy was very sorry that the book had ever been printed. Near the end of her life, she admitted in an interview, "There was a time that I thought I had a lifetime job cut out for me — to track down every copy of the novel and destroy them all, one by one. I used to lie in bed thinking about the book in all the libraries, and once I even tried to find out how many libraries there are in the country. I knew, of course, that most of them had better things to do with their funds than buy a novel from an unknown writer, but the book was in a few libraries, and my hope was to get rid of it as completely as I could."

At the time, however, the book gave Dorothy one of the things she most wanted: money, enough to live on so that she could go on writing. The motion-picture rights to *The Eleventh Virgin* sold to Hollywood for $5,000 — a lavish sum by the standards of the day. Suddenly Dorothy had the freedom that money could buy. As much as she loved New Orleans, she was ready for a change again. (Her friend Mary had already moved back to Chicago.) She moved back to New York, to be reunited with old friends and to try to sort out how she should spend the rest of her life.

CHAPTER 4

The Cottage by the Sea

In New York, Dorothy moved in with her old friend Peggy Baird, who was at that time married to the poet Malcolm Cowley. The Cowleys introduced Dorothy to their circle of literary friends, including novelists John Dos Passos and Caroline Gordon, critic Kenneth Burke, and poets Allen Tate and Hart Crane. Dorothy had always considered herself to be a writer, but she was primarily a journalist. Sometimes she felt overwhelmed by the deep literary discussions that swirled around her. On one occasion, she said later, she listened to a long conversation between Cowley, Burke, and Dos Passos, not understanding a single word.

The Cowleys also introduced Dorothy to an earnest young biologist named Forster Batterham. Forster (he pronounced his name *Foster*) was the son of British parents. He had grown up in North Carolina, the only boy among seven sisters. Like Dorothy, he was deeply concerned about the injustices he saw around him. He

44

considered himself an anarchist, one who believes that all forms of government are inherently evil and should be abolished. With his profound mistrust of man-made institutions, he turned instead to the natural world. He loved the sea and all its creatures with a consuming passion.

In the spring of 1924, Dorothy used most of her Hollywood money to purchase a beach cottage at the western end of Staten Island. The house was tiny, little more than a fisherman's shack with a tin roof. It was so primitive that it did not even have hot water. But from the porch Dorothy could watch the waves, the gulls, and the passing ships. The cottage was a haven of peace where she hoped she could do some serious writing.

Forster, who had a job in the city, spent every weekend with Dorothy at the cottage. He didn't believe in either civil or religious marriage, but eventually he agreed to enter into a common-law union. The two of them would share their lives as fully as any convention-ally married couple, though they had no legal or church sanction.

For the first time in her life, Dorothy was truly happy. She loved Forster deeply, and she cherished every mo-ment of the life they built together. Dorothy had always been a city person. Now Forster opened a spectacular new world to her, a world of currents and tide pools, shells and coral and seabirds. They decorated their living room with dried horseshoe crabs, a donkey's jawbone, birds' nests, and the shell of a sea turtle. There were always books stacked in the corners, and the furniture was festooned with fishing line spread out to dry.

Dorothy continued to earn money through her writing. She published articles on gardening and produced serialized romances for magazines. She also kept a journal, describing her everyday life in vivid detail. In front of the cottage was "a big expanse of rocky wasteland buried in color, mottled with green and red seaweed. It is a paradise for children, though hard on their bare feet. They grow accustomed to it, however, and can soon learn to walk lightly among the stones, finding all kinds of crabs and little fish and eels caught in the pools at low tide. Old men, gaunt and weatherbeaten, come from miles around to dig bait, bending for hours over their digging forks. . . . I go down to the bait-diggers and pick up clams as they turn them up in their search for worms. . . . The waves, the gulls, and the cawing of the crows in the woods behind the house are the only sounds on these days. . . . Up and down the beach, the swells roll in from the ocean, smashing dull and ominous on the sand. But here the waves are gentle and playful."

Forster was not very sociable, but Dorothy quickly made friends with their neighbors. She spent long hours over cups of strong tea with Freda and Sasha, who told her about their lives in their native Russia. Lefty, the beachcomber, expounded his philosophy of life: Why should he work, he asked, when he only spent his

earnings on liquor and wound up in debt to the bootleg-
ger? When the Cowleys bought a cottage of their own
down the beach, Dorothy frequently dropped by to visit
them. She admired Peggy's garden, played with her cats,
and sometimes enjoyed the pure luxury of a hot bath.

Although they were two very different people,
Dorothy and Forster generally got along well. Only one
thing sent Forster into a rage — Dorothy's fascination
with religion. He was teaching her everything he could
about the natural world; why, he demanded, did she
persist in turning to the supernatural?

Yet to Dorothy, the wonders of the sea were evidence
of divine creation. In fact, since moving to the cottage,
she had started to read the Bible again, and she had
been thinking more about God. Happy in the experience of human love, she felt more profoundly than ever
that she was blessed by the love of God. God had given
her the beach, the waves, the community of friends that
surrounded her, and the chance to love and be loved
by this good man. She found herself longing for closeness with God more intensely than ever before. Happy
as she was, she sensed that a still greater happiness
awaited her, if only she could reach it somehow.

In her happiness, she wanted to give thanks to God.
Yet when she tried to kneel and pray, she found herself
swept by doubts. Did she really believe in a supreme
being? After all, the Communists called religion an
opiate, a drug that lulled people into passivity and kept
them from rebelling against oppression. Nevertheless,

prayer came to her as the inevitable outpouring of her happiness. In her journal she described her conflicting feelings:

I am surprised that I am beginning to pray daily. I began because I had to. I just found myself praying. I can't get down on my knees, but I can pray while I am walking. If I get down on my knees I think, "Do I really believe? Whom am I praying to?" And a terrible doubt comes over me, and a sense of shame, and I wonder if I am praying because I am lonely, because I am unhappy.

But when I am walking up to the village for the mail, I find myself praying again, holding the rosary in my pocket that Mary Gordon gave me in New Orleans two years ago.

Then I think suddenly, scornfully, "Here you are in a stupor of content. You are biological. Like a cow. Prayer with you is like the opiate of the people." And over and over again in my mind that phrase is repeated jeeringly, "Religion is the opiate of the people."

"But," I reason with myself, "I am praying because I am happy, not because I am unhappy. I did not turn to God in unhappiness, in grief, in despair, to get consolation, to get something from Him."

And encouraged that I am praying because I want to thank Him, I go on praying. No matter how dull the day, how long the walk seems, if I feel low at the beginning of the walk, the words I have been saying have insinuated themselves into my heart before I have done, so that on the trip back I neither pray nor think but am filled with exultation.

In the early summer of 1925, Dorothy felt that her exultation was nearly complete. At the age of twenty-nine, she was going to have a baby.

Ever since her abortion in New York, Dorothy had feared that she would never be able to bear a child. "The longing in my heart for a baby had been growing," she wrote in her autobiography. "My home, I felt, was not a home without one. The simple joys of the kitchen and garden and beach brought sadness with them because I felt myself unfruitful, barren. No matter how much one was loved or one loved, that love was lonely without a child. It was incomplete."

Dorothy realized that she was pregnant on a brilliant day in June. The circus had come to town, and so Dorothy and Forster, along with Peggy and Malcolm Cowley, packed a picnic lunch and went to see the show. As they enjoyed their pickled eels and bread, their popcorn and root beer, Dorothy felt supremely happy.

But when Dorothy told Forster the news, he was appalled at the idea of having a child. He couldn't forget the horrors of the First World War. It seemed unthinkable to him to bring a new life into such a troubled world. Furthermore, Forster despised the notion of controlling another person's life, even that of a child; he couldn't imagine making rules and enforcing discipline.

He felt that he, of all men, was most unsuited to be a father.

Forster's concerns didn't worry Dorothy very much. She sensed that he would love their child when it arrived, just as he loved all innocent, natural creatures. She passed a quiet summer, gardening, writing, reading, and walking on the beach. In the winter, as the baby's birth drew nearer, she moved back into the city, where she could be close to her sister, Della. Her daughter was born at Bellevue Hospital on March 4, 1926. Dorothy named her Tamar Teresa. The name *Tamar* came from a Hebrew word meaning "little palm tree." Dorothy chose "Teresa" as the baby's middle name in honor of her favorite saint, Teresa of Ávila. It was Saint Teresa who once described life as "a night spent in an uncomfortable inn."

Dorothy was enraptured by her brand-new daughter. In "Having a Baby," an article for the Socialist paper *The New Masses*, she wrote ecstatically, "Tamar Teresa's nose is twisted slightly to one side. She sleeps with the placidity of a Mona Lisa, so that you cannot see the amazing blue of her eyes, which are strangely blank and, occasionally, ludicrously crossed. What little hair she has is auburn and her eyebrows are golden. Her complexion is a rich tan. Her ten fingers and toes are of satisfactory length and slenderness and I reflect that she will be a dancer when she grows up, which future will relieve her of the necessity for learning reading, writing and arithmetic. Her long upper lip, which resembles that of an Irish policeman, may interfere with her beauty but with such posy hands as she has already, nothing will interfere with her grace." Dorothy felt that the wonder of having a baby was a universal experience, shared by rich and poor alike. She wrote of it in a spirit of celebration.

Just as she had hoped, Forster was delighted with Tamar. He loved to watch her as she slept, to play with her when she woke up, to marvel over each of her new accomplishments. But when Dorothy announced that she wanted to have Tamar baptized, Forster raised an invisible wall between them. "I knew that I was going to have my child baptized, cost what it may," Dorothy explained in her autobiography. "I knew that I was not going to have her floundering through many years as I had done, doubting and hesitating, undisciplined and amoral. I felt it was the greatest thing I could do for my child."

Forster had no patience with Dorothy's religious leanings. In his view, the world followed strict, scientific principles that could be measured and understood. Yet Dorothy sensed that Forster would lose respect for her if she ever yielded to his way of thinking. Forster hated hypocrisy in any form. Above all things, he believed that each individual should follow his or her convictions.

Like Forster, Dorothy's Socialist friends were dismayed when she told them that she wanted to raise Tamar in the Catholic Church. One friend even suggested that she should see a psychiatrist, that her yearning toward God was a sign of mental illness. People reminded her that the Church was aligned with the rich and powerful. It devoured the pitiful earnings of the poor and did little to ease their sufferings. Dorothy knew that these criticisms were valid. But she saw the Catholic Church as the church of the masses. As she tried to fathom her own decision, she recognized that the church brought its humblest followers close to the splendor of the Creator. As she wrote later, "In the midst of misery and class strife, life was shot through with glory. Mrs. Barrett in her sordid little tenement flat finished her breakfast dishes at ten o'clock in the morning and got down on her knees and prayed to God." She wanted the Roman Catholic faith to be at the center of her daughter's life.

One day, as she walked to town wheeling Tamar in her stroller, Dorothy passed an elderly nun on the road. Impulsively, she stopped her and asked an urgent question. As a non-Catholic, what must she do to have her daughter baptized in the church?

The nun was Sister Aloysia, who lived and worked at St. Joseph's Home, a nearby Catholic orphanage. She didn't seem at all startled by Dorothy's question. She explained that Dorothy must study the catechism, a series of lessons on church dogma, before Tamar's baptism could be arranged. She, Sister Aloysia, would be her teacher.

True to her word, Sister Aloysia appeared three times a week at Dorothy's cottage. The catechism was a series of questions that the Sister expected Dorothy to repeat and answer by rote. There was no discussion of church history or the pope's position on social issues. Still, Dorothy felt content to learn the words of the catechism by heart, confident that understanding would dawn in due time.

If Dorothy stumbled through her lesson, Sister Aloysia became angry. "And you think you are intelligent!" she would cry. "What is the definition of grace — actual grace and sanctifying grace? My fourth-grade pupils know more than you do!" Obediently, Dorothy would study harder until she knew the lesson perfectly.

As Dorothy's spiritual teacher, Sister Aloysia took it upon herself to try to whip Dorothy's entire life into shape. "Here you sit at your typewriter at ten o'clock and none of your dishes done yet!" she scolded. "Supper and breakfast dishes besides! And why don't you [clean] your ceiling? It's all dirty from wood smoke!" She worried that Tamar might die before her baptism could take place, and she fretted that the baby wasn't bundled up warmly enough against the sea breezes.

Most of all, Sister Aloysia was concerned with the state of Dorothy's soul. How, she asked again and again, could Dorothy have her child baptized without becoming a Catholic herself? But Dorothy was not yet ready to take that final step in her own life. She knew that if she became a member of the Catholic Church, she would lose Forster forever. She could not continue to live with him unless they were married in the eyes of God. Yet she had been married before, and the Church did not recognize divorce. Even if they could somehow jump that hurdle, she knew that Forster would never accept a religious ceremony to make them man and wife.

When she came to the door, Sister Aloysia always peered about her apprehensively and asked, "Is *he* here?" She wouldn't enter the house if Forster was there. In fact, Forster made no effort to hide his hostility toward the catechism classes. And as Dorothy went on with her studies, he was at home less and less. He spent long hours in his boat or fishing from the end of the pier. Some nights he didn't come home at all, but wrapped himself in his coat and slept on the beach.

In July, when she was four months old, Tamar Teresa was baptized at last. Afterward Dorothy invited a group of friends to the beach house for a small party to celebrate, and she served lobsters that Forster had caught in his traps for the occasion. But Forster didn't stay to enjoy the feast. Angry and distraught, he disappeared for several days. "It was his protest against my yearnings toward the life of the spirit," Dorothy wrote later, "which he considered a morbid escapism."

Over the following year, Forster left Dorothy many times. Always he returned, and each time she welcomed him back. But the struggle — their loving each other yet growing further and further apart — took a terrible toll on them both. Forster grew more moody and distant than ever, and Dorothy developed a series of strange physical symptoms. At night she awoke choking, unable to breathe. After she underwent a battery of tests, the doctors told her that she suffered from a "nervous condition." Her illness was the result of the continual stress she was enduring.

Finally, in December of 1927, Forster left again, but when he returned this time, Dorothy refused to let him back into the house. The decision was agony, yet she felt compelled to make it. "My heart was breaking with my own determination to make an end, once and for all, to the torture we were undergoing," she wrote in her autobiography.

The next day, December 28, 1927, Dorothy was baptized at the Catholic church in the Staten Island village of Tottenville. After her baptism, she made her confession and took the sacrament of Holy Communion for the first time. Yet she experienced no surge of joy, no uplifting religious fervor. Even now, as she took this final step that had been so long in coming, she felt torn by doubt. In *The Long Loneliness* she recalled, "One part of my mind stood at one side and kept saying, 'What are you doing? Are you sure of yourself? What kind of an affectation is this? What act is this you are going through? Are you trying to induce emotion, induce faith, partake of an opiate, the opiate of the people?'"

Dorothy had known the deepest joy that human love could bring to her life. Now she had sacrificed that happiness in search of a love that was even more profound, more wondrous. She had gained the church, but she had paid a terrible price.

CHAPTER 5

A Prayer and an Answer

After her baptism, Dorothy determined to begin a new life, a life dedicated to God. She closed the beach house and moved back to New York City. She rented a spacious West Side apartment with a magnificent open fireplace, and supported herself and Tamar by writing articles and synopses of novels for MGM Studios. The work was thoroughly worldly, but it helped to pay the bills and gave her time for more spiritual explorations. Faithfully she attended Mass and went to confession. Father Zachary, the elderly parish priest, took a special interest in her religious education. He gave her books that helped her gain a deeper understanding of Catholic doctrine. Father Zachary was also interested in her writing career. After he read several of her articles and short stories, he complained that they were too dull and grim. Still, when Dorothy was leaving the confessional, he would often whisper, "Sold any more stories lately?"

Dorothy was now free from any lingering religious doubts. She felt strong and certain in her faith, and she didn't regret her decision to become a Catholic. Yet she was not content simply to be a member of the church. As she explained years later, "My conversion was a way of saying to myself that I knew I was trying to go someplace, and that I would spend the rest of my life trying to go there, and trying not to let myself get distracted by side trips, excursions that were not to the point." She wanted to merge her religious beliefs with her commitment to social action, which remained as powerful as ever. Yet, as hard as she searched, the Catholic Church did not show her the way.

In the summer of 1929, Dorothy was surprised by a call from a Hollywood motion-picture company. They had seen a play that she had sent to MGM a while ago. Would she come to Los Angeles to write dialogue for the movies? By September, Dorothy and Tamar were in California, and she had begun her new job. She had high hopes, as she explained in her autobiography: "Like all Hollywood-bound authors, I thought of the money that I would make that would free me for a simple life in the future and for work on the novel I was always writing."

But Dorothy's hopes were dashed. She quickly discovered that Hollywood was neither glamorous nor exciting. Everything cost more than she expected. Although she was well paid, her salary barely covered food, rent, and Tamar's day care. The work was dull and often seemed pointless. Worst of all, she was inconsolably lonely. She longed for a community of friends, people who shared her goals and passions. She experienced again that sense of "long loneliness" that she believed afflicted women particularly. As she explained it, "I found out so many times, over and over again, that women especially are social beings, who are not content with just husband and family, but must have a community, a group, an exchange with others. A child is not enough. A husband and children, no matter how busy one may be kept by them, are not enough. Young and old, even in the busiest years of our lives, we women especially are victims of the long loneliness."

After three months, Dorothy's Hollywood contract ran out. She was reluctant to go back to New York, where she might be tempted to seek out Forster again. Instead she embarked on a fresh adventure and headed for Mexico City.

The Catholic Church had long been a major force in Mexico. Now, in 1930, Mexico's government was trying to strip the church of its power. With her skills as a reporter, Dorothy was in a good position to tell the world about Mexico's anticlerical activities. She and Tamar lived with a poor Mexican family, and Dorothy wrote a series of articles for the Catholic magazine *Commonweal*.

Dorothy was entranced by Mexico. She loved its birds and flowers, its joyous festivals, the strength and dignity of its people. But during the summer Tamar became ill. So Dorothy and Tamar left Mexico to spend some time with Dorothy's parents, who were living in Florida. As soon as they returned to the United States, Tamar's health improved dramatically.

For the next two years, Dorothy drifted from Florida to New York and from one job to another. By the summer of 1932 she had rented an apartment on East Fifteenth Street in Manhattan, which she shared with her younger brother John and his Argentine wife, Tessa. Like Dorothy, both John and Tessa were deeply committed to fighting social injustice.

In 1932, the United States was in the throes of the worst economic depression in its history. Banks and factories shut down. Millions of unemployed men and women waited in line for handouts of bread and soup. Hoboes rode in boxcars from town to town, looking for whatever work they could find. But despite the misery around her, Dorothy spent a tranquil summer of reading and writing. She began work on another novel, using the Great Depression as its background. But she never completed the book. She was thirty-five years old, and she still felt that her life had no consuming purpose.

In December of 1932, thousands of unemployed workers traveled to Washington, D.C., to stage a demonstration. The "Hunger Marchers" hoped to make the public and the legislators more aware of their plight. The demonstration was organized by the Unemployed Workers' Council, a group that had Communist backing. But few of the demonstrators had Communist leanings. They were ordinary people, driven to desperation by hard times.

Dorothy was thrilled when she learned about the demonstration, and she set out for the capital to write a story for *Commonweal*. Most of the nation's newspapers ran stories of the "Communist menace," churning up the public's worst fears. For three days, squadrons of policemen prevented the marchers from entering the city. The demonstrators waited patiently, camping in their battered trucks or sleeping beside the road in the December cold.

Then, at last, permission for the march was granted, and the demonstrators poured into the streets. Dorothy described the scene in her autobiography: "On a bright sunny day the ragged horde, triumphantly with banners flying, with lettered slogans mounted on sticks, paraded three thousand strong through the tree-flanked streets of Washington." For Dorothy, watching from the sidelines, it was a moment of victory, but a time of sadness as well: "I stood on the curb and watched them, joy and pride in the courage of this band of men and women mounting in my heart, and with it a bitterness too that since I was now a Catholic, with fundamental philosophical differences, I could not be out there with them. I could write, I could protest, to arouse the conscience, but where was the Catholic leadership in the gathering of bands of men and women together, for the actual works of mercy that the comrades had always made part of their technique in reaching the workers?"

Weren't there any alternatives? Dorothy asked herself. Did she have no choices besides Communism and capitalism? Was there no way for her as a Christian to fight the system that oppressed the poor?

When the demonstration was over, Dorothy took the opportunity to go to the national shrine at Washington's Catholic University. There, during the Feast of the Immaculate Conception, she offered up a heartfelt prayer. With tears streaming down her face, she asked God to point out a way for her to use her talents for the good of humankind, for the poor. She prayed that her life would be given a guiding purpose.

When she returned to New York, John and Tessa announced that a stranger had come in search of her while she was away. He had promised to return, for he urgently wished to speak with her. His name was Peter Maurin.

Dorothy had been home for only a few hours when she heard a knock at the door. The man who stepped inside was short and broad-shouldered, with a weather-beaten face and warm gray eyes. His collar was dirty, and his crumpled gray suit looked as though he had slept in it; Dorothy learned later that indeed he had. He was fifty-five years old, although he looked still older. Tessa explained that this was Peter Maurin, who had come looking for Dorothy while she was away.

Almost at once Peter began to talk as though he were picking up a conversation that had been interrupted just minutes before. He made a brief comment about Dorothy's recent trip to the nation's capital. Then, in a thick French accent, he began, "People go to Washington asking the government to solve their economic problems, while the federal government was never intended to solve men's economic problems. Thomas Jefferson says that the less government there is the better it is. If the less government there is, the better it is, then the best kind of government is self-government."

Six-year-old Tamar called from the next room. She had come down with the measles while Dorothy was gone, and now she wanted her mother's attention. But Peter Maurin went on talking. "If the best kind of government is self-government, then the best kind of organization is self-organization. When the organizers try to organize the unorganized, then the organizers don't organize themselves. And when the organizers don't organize themselves, nobody organizes himself. And when nobody organizes himself, nothing is organized."

Peter never seemed to pause for breath. Dorothy listened in amazement. At last she excused herself and went into Tamar's room. Peter followed her, still talking without a break.

Soon the doctor arrived to check on Tamar's progress. As he bent over the bed, taking Tamar's temperature, Peter Maurin began talking to him as well. When the plumber appeared to fix a leaky pipe, and the gas man came to read the meter, Peter followed them through the apartment, pursuing them with his endless barrage of words.

Dorothy was exhausted after her trip. She wanted to

spend time with Tamar, whom she hadn't seen in several days. Yet at the same time, she found Peter Maurin strangely fascinating. Somehow, through her confusion and astonishment, she sensed that he had ideas to share, ideas that would prove important.

Peter Maurin had been born in 1877 in the French province of Languedoc, the oldest in an enormous peasant family of twenty-three children. The Maurins had farmed the same parcel of land for nearly fifteen hundred years. Following an ancient tradition, the families in the neighborhood all baked their bread in one large community oven and pastured their sheep on common grazing land.

When Peter was twelve, he left the farm and made the journey to Paris, the first city he had ever seen. There he attended a school for peasant boys, run by an order of monks called the Christian Brothers. After five years of study, he became a teacher at the school. But, as he told Dorothy, "I was always interested in the land and in men's life on the land," and some years later he was lured away by the promise of land and opportunity in Canada. For two years he and a partner worked a homestead in the Canadian wilderness. But when his partner died in a hunting accident, Peter gave up the homestead and went on the road. For a while he drifted across Canada, hiring on with work gangs to cut timber or harvest crops. Then in 1911 he entered the United States.

In the States, Peter continued to drift from job to job. He worked on farms, in brickyards, and in steel mills. In Chicago he went into business for a while as a teacher of French. Wherever he was, he read constantly. When he moved on to another town, his suitcase wasn't full of clothes; it was heavy with his ever-growing collection of books.

From Chicago, Peter moved on to New York. For seven years he worked at a Catholic boys' camp in the Catskill Mountains north of the city. He earned a dollar a day and slept in the barn, which he shared with an elderly horse. But he was perfectly satisfied with his living conditions. Through his ceaseless reading, he had formed a clear philosophy about the important things in life. Voluntary poverty, the stripping away of unnecessary material goods, was one of his ideals.

During his years at the boys' camp, Peter made frequent trips to New York City, where he spent happy hours reading in the public library. He also discovered Union Square, a park on Fourteenth Street that had long been popular with labor leaders, Communists, and other radicals. Peter became one of the Union Square regulars. At any time of day, in any season, he could always find someone to listen to his ideas.

Peter had ideas about everything, and he spread them like a farmer sowing seeds across a field. He deplored the materialism of the modern world and talked of the higher spiritual values that would free humankind from cruelty and greed. He believed that most people were too concerned with promoting their own personal gain. To build a better society, people must learn to work together for the common good. They must share their resources, as the French peasants of his youth had shared their oven and their grazing land.

If people were not sure how to proceed, Peter pointed out, they had only to study the teachings of Christ. Jesus had explained it all. Through true Christian love, individuals could rebuild the world. It was a matter of "seeing Christ in others, loving the Christ you saw in others. Greater than this, it was having faith in the Christ in others without being able to see Him."

As the years passed, Peter became convinced that he must start a newspaper that would send his ideas out into the world. But he couldn't do the work alone. He needed a disciple, someone who would understand his ideas, recognize their value, and carry them forward.

Whenever he collared a stranger in Union Square, Peter mentioned his idea about a newspaper. One day he met George Shuster, an editor at *Commonweal*, the Catholic paper that had printed Dorothy's story about the Washington hunger march. Shuster suggested that if Peter wanted to found a radical paper, he ought to talk to Dorothy Day.

When Dorothy first met Peter Maurin at her Fifteenth Street apartment, she was too tired and overwhelmed to absorb much of what he was saying. Several months passed before she realized that he was the answer to her prayer at the national shrine in Washington. Peter Maurin, the French peasant in the crumpled suit, would finally give her life the purpose she was seeking.

CHAPTER 6

A Penny a Copy

Every day when Dorothy came home from work, Peter Maurin was there to greet her. He gave her no peace. He talked to her as she unpacked the groceries, cooked supper, and washed the dishes. One night, Dorothy and Tessa wanted to listen to a symphony on the radio. Dorothy begged Peter to be quiet, just for an hour. "He did his best," she recalled, "but sooner or later his face started working, his eyes lit up, his nose twitched, his finger began to mark out points in the air before him. . . . Finally, when he could bear it no longer, he looked at me wistfully and then, seeing my adamant expression, turned to Tessa. I remember that night especially because he went over and knelt down by her chair and began whispering to her, unable to restrain himself longer."

Peter was dismayed by the limited Catholic education that Dorothy had received from Sister Aloysia. Even the books that Father Zachary had given her to read had not been enough; she still had significant gaps in her education. Immediately Peter set about to correct the situation. He encouraged her to read the lives of the saints and the writings of leading Catholic scholars. He told her about the papal encyclicals, a series of statements issued by the Roman Catholic popes over the centuries. The encyclicals interpreted the teachings of Jesus to mean that Catholics had a responsibility to help others, to take action against evil and injustice in the world. The Church had not been silent on social issues after all. This was the Catholic call to action that Dorothy had longed to hear.

Often Peter brought friends to the apartment with him — people he met in Union Square, at Columbus Circle on West 59th Street, or on the subway. There was Klein, a young Jewish Socialist who was astounded by the casual way that Dorothy and Peter spoke of God. There was Dan Irwin, an unemployed bookkeeper. There was Frank O'Donnell, a salesman with a troubled conscience: he used pressure tactics to sell family photographs to poor people. There was a man who sold gardenias on the street, and a college student who was arrested regularly for sleeping in Central Park.

Not all of Peter's friends were destitute. Sometimes powerful men from the upper classes were impressed by his ideas and wanted to hear more. Now and then he brought along Thomas Woodlock, an editor of the *Wall Street Journal,* or John Moody of Moody's Investments.

The apartment on Fifteenth Street buzzed with talk.

Dorothy had few quiet moments; privacy was almost unknown. But there was always another place at the table, a fresh pot of coffee. Everyone was made welcome.

The coming of Peter Maurin meant big changes for Tamar. Suddenly strangers were trooping through the apartment, and her mother seemed distracted by all the talk and confusion. Sometimes in the evening Dorothy would settle Tamar in her bath and return to her guests in the kitchen. Tamar would stay in the tub, splashing and playing happily until the water grew cold. Having Peter around meant that she could stay up late, because no one remembered to send her to bed.

Gradually over the months, Dorothy absorbed Peter's ideas. He talked a great deal about Francis of Assisi, the saint who gave up worldly riches "out of the fullness of his heart." Saint Francis was Peter's ideal — humble and generous, asking nothing and giving all. Peter felt that true freedom lay in this "voluntary poverty." His ideas echoed Dorothy's own early desire to live among the poor as one of them.

Peter believed that modern society was in serious trouble because it had lost its spiritual dimension. Instead, it stressed materialism — the piling up of goods and money. Mediocrity was on the rise. "There is no such thing as historical progress," he often exclaimed. "The present is in no wise an improvement over the past. . . . The will to power, to well-being, to wealth triumphs over the will to holiness, to genius."

But Peter Maurin did not despair. He believed that

people were eager to change, that they hungered for spiritual meaning in their lives. He was convinced that a new order could emerge, a world in which "it will be easier for people to be good."

As she took in Peter's ideas, Dorothy felt a dawning excitement. Peter envisioned a world fueled not by wealth and power but by the spirit of Christian love flowing from one individual to another. Dorothy was eager to turn his words into reality, to show what could be achieved by following Christ's teachings.

The talks at Dorothy's apartment marked the beginning of Peter Maurin's program for changing the world. First, he proposed, there must be round-table discussions for the "clarification of thought." These discussions would help people focus upon the important ideas that would be the basis for direct action. This direct action would involve developing farming communes where people would live and work together on the land, and opening "houses of hospitality" in the cities, places where the destitute could receive food, shelter, and comfort. And getting the word out about these programs would involve creating a newspaper unlike any that had ever been published before, a Catholic paper of radical ideas.

Of all Peter's proposals, it was the notion of a newspaper that captured Dorothy's imagination. This was far from surprising. Dorothy's father was a newspaperman, and her three brothers were all involved in newspaper work. Sam worked for the New York *Journal-*

American; Donald was a writer with the New York *Tribune*; and her younger brother, John, was involved with various Socialist papers. Dorothy herself was an experienced journalist. Here at last was a way for her to use her talents for the good of humanity. A Catholic paper would bring together her Christian faith, her commitment to the poor, and her love for the written word.

But it cost money to put out a paper, and she and Peter had no funds. "In the history of the saints," Peter said, "capital was raised by prayer. God sends you what you need when you need it. You will be able to pay the printer. Just read the lives of the saints."

Dorothy thought about what Peter said. She had a typewriter, some paper, and a kitchen table. She had plenty of ideas for articles. The Paulist Press, a small Catholic publishing company, agreed to print 2,500 copies of a four-page tabloid for $57. Dorothy had $57, but it was set aside to pay rent, as well as the gas and electric bills.

She wouldn't worry about the bills, she decided. The paper must come first, and the rest would take care of itself.

Little by little, money trickled in. A church pastor donated ten dollars. A nun gave a dollar. Dorothy received fifteen dollars for an article she had written. As though by magic, the bills were soon paid.

As they worked at the kitchen table, Peter, Dorothy, and Dorothy's brother John debated over what the new paper should be called. Peter wanted to call it *The Catholic Radical*. But Dorothy, with her dedication to the labor movement, preferred *The Catholic Worker*. "Man proposes, but woman disposes," Peter said cheerfully. The paper was called *The Catholic Worker* forever after. Sold for a penny a copy, it was affordable to even the poorest of the unemployed. Over the decades that followed, as the United States witnessed soaring inflation, the price of *The Catholic Worker* never changed.

In the Soviet Union and in many other countries throughout the world, May 1 is a holiday in honor of the worker. So Dorothy thought it fitting that the *The Catholic Worker* begin publication on May 1, 1933. The first issue ran articles condemning child labor, racial inequality, and the plight of West Virginia coal miners. In her editorial Dorothy explained who the paper was for: "For those who are sitting on park benches in the warm spring sunlight. For those who are huddling in shelters trying to escape the rain. For those who are walking the streets in the all but futile search for work. For those who think that there is no hope for the future, no recognition of their plight — this little paper is addressed. It is printed to call their attention to the fact that the Catholic Church has a social program — to let them know that there are men of God who are working not only for their spiritual but for their material welfare."

Early on the morning of May 1, Dorothy and three young volunteers set out to peddle *The Catholic Worker*. They hauled their bundles of papers to Union Square, where about 50,000 people had gathered for a huge Communist rally. "Read *The Catholic Worker!*" they cried, edging their way through a sea of banners and placards. "A penny a copy!"

The word *Catholic* was not popular in Communist circles. Dorothy and her assistants were bombarded with jeers. Yet they sold hundreds of papers. Each time a hand reached out for *The Catholic Worker,* Dorothy felt a glow of triumph. By the end of the day, she was exultant. *The Catholic Worker* was off to a glorious start.

Peter, however, had reservations. He feared that *The Catholic Worker* was too much like *The Daily Worker,* the widely distributed Communist paper. Its call for social action was too political for his taste, lacking the spiritual content he felt was essential. He wanted the paper to express the philosophy which he called "personalism," the belief that the only way to change society was through the personal action of each individual. "Everybody's paper is nobody's paper," he grumbled.

Peter was also disappointed that Dorothy had printed few of his articles. He had pictured a paper that would be strictly a forum for his own ideas. Dorothy assured him that she wanted to print some of Peter's essays in every issue, but she felt that other people must have a chance to express their thoughts as well. Peter was so upset that he left New York and returned to the camp in the Catskills, with its barn and his friend the aging horse.

But by the middle of May, Peter was back, carrying

a new stack of books. He began talking again, as though no time had elapsed. He bore Dorothy no hard feelings, but he resigned from his position as "contributing editor." He explained that the paper was bound to publish articles with which he disagreed, and he didn't want to be responsible for them. Dorothy assured him that the paper would print some of his pieces in every issue.

It was Dorothy's brother John who came up with a name for Peter's articles. He called them "Easy Essays," although they were not really easy at all. Written in short phrases so that they looked like poetry on the printed page, they dealt with life's biggest issues. One essay read as follows:

The world would be better off
if people tried to become better,
and people would become better
if they stopped trying to become better off.
For when everyone tries to become better off
nobody is better off.
But when everyone tries to become better
everybody is better off.
Everyone would be rich if nobody tried to become richer,
and nobody would be poor if everybody tried to be the poorest.
And everybody would be what he ought to be if everybody tried to be
what he wants the other fellow to be.

That summer, seven-year-old Tamar went to stay with her Aunt Della, and John and Tessa moved to a small town on the Hudson River. Meanwhile, Dorothy concentrated on *The Catholic Worker*. Donations continued to trickle in from priests, nuns, and interested readers. There was never much money to spare, but she managed to keep the paper going from month to month. The third issue ran to 10,000 copies.

In the paper's first issue, Dorothy began a column that would appear monthly for more than forty years. At first she called it "The Listener." Later it was headed "Day after Day," and for a time, "Day by Day." Finally, in 1946, Dorothy found the name that suited her best. She called her column "On Pilgrimage." A series of musings on the large and small events of her everyday life, it reflected her personal journey toward spiritual fulfillment.

The paper quickly outgrew the kitchen of the Fifteenth Street apartment. So Dorothy rented an empty barbershop downstairs where she and Peter could set up operations. Behind the shop was an enclosed patio, ideal for Peter's round-table discussions. On warm summer evenings, people drifted in from the streets to drink tea and listen to lectures by priests, rabbis, and college professors. Afterward there were long discussions, which sometimes turned into heated arguments. Dorothy recalled one especially lively evening when "a Russian doctor, a German Benedictine priest, and a Mexican general were there all talking at once, each espousing his particular cause in his own accent. The Russian favored theocracy; the German priest talked of 'victim souls'; and the Mexican, inflamed by the persecutions then going on, wanted us to help raise arms for a counter-revolution. Peter, in the interests of clarification of thought, talked in his French accent of farming communes."

No matter how much the paper grew, Dorothy never ran it like a traditional business. Early in 1934 she reported in her journal that the printer had called, demanding an overdue payment. "We told him he had better get busy and pray for it right now," she wrote.

Twice a year in *The Catholic Worker,* Dorothy appealed for financial contributions. Some of her friends urged her to open a bank account and make interest-bearing investments that would put the venture on more solid ground. But Dorothy didn't want to invest in corporations that oppressed the workers. "This isn't a business, it's a movement," she protested. "And we don't know anything about business around here anyway. . . . Probably most of our friends live as we do, from day to day and from hand to mouth, and as they get, they are willing to give. So we shall continue to appeal and we know that the paper will go on."

CHAPTER 7

House of Hospitality

One day during the summer of 1933, Peter Maurin met a pair of ragged unemployed men in Union Square. Dolan and Egan, as they called themselves, listened closely while Peter talked. He nicknamed them "the workers," and he hoped that they would be among his first disciples.

To Peter, the world's homeless drifters were all "ambassadors of Christ." As he had done many times before, he brought his new friends to the house on East Fifteenth Street. Dolan and Egan enjoyed the hot meals and endless cups of coffee that Dorothy provided. In fact, they felt so comfortable that they dropped by nearly every day. Knocking on the door, they would announce, "Dolan and Egan here again!"

As usual, Dorothy tried to be a welcoming hostess. But she was busy with *The Catholic Worker,* and sometimes she resented the intrusion. It became a joke among her personal friends, who would call cheerfully,

76

"Dolan and Egan here again!" when they stopped in for a visit.

Dorothy was never sure whether Dolan and Egan caught on to Peter's philosophy. But they did make themselves useful by selling *The Catholic Worker*. They kept the pennies they earned to buy "eats and tobacco."

Much of the paper's sales force consisted of students like the young men who had helped Dorothy on May Day. They read the paper and offered to peddle it on the streets. Often they stopped in at Fifteenth Street to hear a lecture and stayed to cook meals and serve the people who crowded into the old barbershop in greater numbers every day.

One such student was Stanley Vishnewski, a seventeen-year-old Lithuanian boy from Brooklyn. He saw Dorothy selling *The Catholic Worker* in Union Square one morning and asked how he could help. "Join us," she told him, and he did. After that he spent his days at Fifteenth Street, or shouting "Read *The Catholic Worker!*" as he walked the pavements. His father urged him to find a steady, respectable job. But Stanley Vishnewski remained with *The Catholic Worker* until his death, forty-five years later.

To young people like Stanley Vishnewski, Dorothy Day and Peter Maurin offered something unique and compelling. Julia Porcelli, who came to *The Catholic Worker* when she was a high-school senior, reflected years later, "As a child I didn't see many people living by faith, and I guess I was very hungry for things of the spirit.

When I read *The Catholic Worker* I guess I felt, well, these are Catholic people. They are doing something for their neighbors. I instinctively felt, as a little old Italian lady [once] told me, 'God has all the grace, but He wants you to use your hands, your feet, your time, and your brain.' And this is what Catholic action is."

One evening, a big, burly man arrived at the house on Fifteenth Street, roaring and groaning in distress. When Dorothy asked how they could help him, he bellowed that he had been walking all day in search of work and needed to soak his feet. Someone brought him a brimming washtub. He pulled off his shoes and dirt-caked socks and lowered his feet into the steaming water with a sigh of contentment. "Big Dan," as he was called, became another regular at the house. With his booming voice, he proved to be one of *The Catholic Worker*'s finest salesmen, peddling the paper through the streets of New York from a horse-drawn wagon.

The Great Depression of the 1930s was a terrible time of joblessness and hunger in the United States. Word spread quickly that the people on Fifteenth Street offered free soup and bread. The Catholic Workers, as Dorothy and her helpers described themselves, began to serve meals in shifts. Many of the people who arrived at mealtimes had lost their homes as well as their jobs. Dorothy would always set up another cot for anyone who needed a place to stay. Several of the Catholic Workers moved into the building too, in order to be of assistance day and night.

Soon the Catholic Workers and their friends were overflowing the Fifteenth Street building. With the help of donations, Dorothy rented an apartment down the block, then half a dozen scattered rooms and apartments in the neighborhood. Finally she packed up the newspaper, the kitchen, her own personal belongings — the whole community — and moved across town to a four-story house on Charles Street in Greenwich Village. Just as Peter Maurin had planned, the Catholic Worker movement had established a "house of hospitality."

Who was Dorothy Day, this woman who gathered such a diverse family about her? Looking back, Julia Porcelli tried to capture her essence in words: "I compared her to Greta Garbo [an early film actress] who was very popular then — Dorothy's beautiful jaw and her features and her coloring, beautiful bone-structure. But more than her looks was her presence. When she enters a room you are very much aware of her. You can't ignore that she's there. There are so few who have this quality." Indeed, Dorothy was an intense presence in any gathering, a woman who swept others into the passion of her own total commitment.

For young people like Stanley and Julia, Catholic action meant more than serving soup and sandwiches to the poor. They wanted to make their voices heard, to try to eliminate the injustices that caused so much poverty and suffering. In 1934, Catholic Workers picketed the Mexican consulate in New York to protest Mexico's suppression of the Roman Catholic Church. The following year, Workers demonstrated in front of the German consulate, protesting the rise of anti-Semitism under Germany's new leader, Adolf Hitler. During a ten-week seamen's strike, Workers were on hand with food and coffee for the strikers. They opened temporary headquarters in a storefront on Tenth Avenue, sometimes serving one thousand men a day.

Peter generally frowned on such activities; "Strikes don't strike me," he commented. As far as he was concerned, higher wages and better working conditions would never change the capitalist system. He wanted to eliminate the money-based economy altogether, to build a world where people would work because they loved their fellow human beings. Although Dorothy accepted his ideas, she also felt that nonviolent demonstrations were an effective way to work for social change. She never abandoned her commitment to the labor movement. When workers went out on strike, they had her sympathy and support.

By 1935, 110,000 copies of *The Catholic Worker* rolled off the presses each month. By now it had developed an extensive mailing list, with subscribers all across the country. The paper's layout and illustrations were eye-catching and attractive. People recognized the masthead — two workers, one black and one white, standing side by side holding picks and shovels. Behind them was the image of Jesus, to show that all people were united in Christ.

Each issue of *The Catholic Worker* carried lively woodcuts by a young artist called Ade Bethune. According to Catholic Worker legend, she had signed her first pictures "A. de Bethune." Someone made an error in setting the type, and her new name stuck. Ade Bethune was a Belgian immigrant with a flair for drawing saints in natural, realistic poses. To her, Joseph really was a carpenter, working with hammer and chisel. Saint Peter was an ordinary fisherman mending tangled nets by the shore. Her drawings helped readers understand that great people could also be humble, and that humble people could be great.

One day an elderly woman named Mary Lane stopped at the Charles Street house with a box of clothes for the poor. Convinced that Dorothy Day must be a very holy person to do such charitable work, she asked her if she had ecstasies and visions. "Hell, no!" Dorothy replied. "The only vision I have is of unpaid bills!" Fortunately, Mary Lane was not put off by Dorothy's bluntness. She had a friend, Gertrude Burke, who owned two adjoining apartment houses on Mott Street in New York's Little Italy section. With a bit of persuasion from Mary Lane, Gertrude Burke agreed to let the Catholic Workers use the rear building if they would collect rents and manage the tenants in the front house.

Dorothy had always loved Little Italy, with its markets and pushcarts and its many churches. But the buildings at 115 Mott Street were in woeful disrepair. She was appalled at the thought of asking anyone to pay rent for the dirty, rundown front apartments. Eventually, however, the Catholic Worker moved into the rear building. Over the next few months, as apartments in the front house fell vacant, the Workers took them over, too. Soon they were using both buildings for the paper, for lectures and discussions, and for the house of hospitality.

Early each morning, hundreds of hungry men stood in line outside the Catholic Worker house, patiently waiting to be served coffee and bread. One Worker wrote a moving description of the breadline for the paper:

> It is easy to recognize the familiar hats, coats, shoes, and other misfitting clothing of the regular comers. All, after being out for hours in the cold, are hunched against the weather and have their hands in their pockets. . . . When I am busy putting peanut butter on bread and can't see their faces I can recognize the arms that reach for bread. One gets to know all the familiar marks of the garments. The hands of some tremble from age, sickness or drink. It is near closing time and the line thins out. They must go out now into a world seemingly full of people whose hearts are as hard and cold as the pavements they must walk all day in quest of their needs. Walk they must for if they sit in the park (when it is warm) the police will shoo them off. Then there is the worry of the next meal or that night's sleeping arrangements. . . . It is awful to think this will start again tomorrow.

Many of the young people who came to the Catholic Worker were aghast at what they found. They were expected to work ten or more hours a day without pay, to live on thin soup and bread, and to sleep in crowded dormitories on ragged mattresses. Some fled in horror from the moans of the sick, the ravings of the mentally ill, and the stench of unwashed bodies. As Stanley Vishnewski later commented, "For a long time the test of a true Catholic Worker . . . was if one could put up with bedbugs."

The poor people who came to Mott Street for food or shelter were not regarded as patients or welfare cases, but as guests. Dealing with them was not always pleasant or rewarding. Many were addicted to alcohol or drugs; some were angry, bitter, and disruptive. Stanley Vishnewski once quipped that the "house of hospitality" ought to be called the "house of hostility." Yet no one was ever turned away from the Catholic Worker house. For Dorothy, the house of hospitality was a chance to put Christian love into practice.

It was easy to feel a kinship with people who were gentle and appreciative, who had fallen on hard times through no fault of their own. It was much harder to recognize that the brawler and the stumbling alcoholic also belonged to the Body of Christ, that they too must be respected and loved. Dorothy felt that the most difficult guests had a vital lesson to impart. In her writing and in her day-to-day work, she emphasized that all human beings, no matter how unlovely, were part of God's creation and therefore members of one community under heaven. "It was human love that helped me to understand divine love," she explained. "Human love at its best, unselfish, glowing, illuminating our days, gives us a glimpse of the love of God for man."

Dorothy believed that the best way to get people to behave well was by setting an example of Christian living. Each guest was treated with kindness and respect. And, although voluntary contributions were certainly welcome, no one was asked to pay for meals or lodging with either money or labor. Predictably, there were always some people who grumbled, quarreled, and sat idle while others toiled on their behalf. "In the real world of Mott Street you could throw good example at some people forever and watch it bounce off them like peanuts off a tank," wrote one Catholic Worker, John Cort. "So a number of useful things did not get done, and some not-so-useful things did get done, because the people setting the good example were greatly outnumbered by the people setting the bad example, or, more likely, just setting." But many guests were deeply grateful for the help they received and eager to give something in return. They chopped vegetables in the kitchen, ran errands, and pitched in when it was time to fold the next batch of *Catholic Workers*.

Dorothy and Peter urged the Catholic Workers to embrace "voluntary poverty." This voluntary giving up of material possessions was not the same as the terrible deprivation which the Workers saw all around them and which they tried to ease as best they could. "We are our brothers' keepers," Dorothy wrote. "Whatever we have beyond our own needs belongs to the poor. If we sow sparingly we will reap sparingly. . . . If we do give in this way, then the increase comes. There will be enough. Somehow we will survive; 'The pot of meal shall not waste, nor the cruze of oil be diminished,' for all our giving away the last bit of substance we have."

As time passed, people around the nation were inspired by the accounts they read of the house on Mott Street. Houses of hospitality sprang up in Chicago, San Francisco, Milwaukee, Cleveland, Pittsburgh, Boston, and Houma, Louisiana. By 1941 there were thirty such houses in the United States and one in England. It was Dorothy's cherished hope that these houses would set an example for people in general, that the actions of the Catholic Workers would offer the world a lesson in giving and love.

CHAPTER 8

Back to the Land

In the winter of 1935, when the Catholic Workers moved to the house on Charles Street, Peter Maurin began to press for the third phase of his plan for social action. It was time, he said, to establish the first farming commune. Peter was convinced that society could never be rebuilt as long as people lived in cities and depended upon machines for their survival. They lived far from the sources of their food and were cut off from spiritual sustenance as well. If the masses of people abandoned the cities and returned to the land, Peter reasoned, families would be strong once more, poverty and crime would disappear, and people would find God at the center of their lives.

Peter referred to his farming communes as "agronomic universities." There scholars would be workers and workers would become scholars. The people living on the farming communes would raise the food they needed for themselves and share their surplus with the houses of hospitality in cities nearby.

Dorothy Day at forty. Her gaze shows both compassion
and determination, two of the qualities she was best
known for as a "friend to the forgotten."
Courtesy of Marquette University Archives

John Day in 1932. Although Dorothy cared about her father, the two of them were never close. He described her as "a nut" when she dedicated herself to the Catholic Worker movement.
Courtesy of Marquette University Archives

Grace Satterlee Day, ca. 1910. Grace was a patient and resourceful woman. The help she gave to others during the San Francisco earthquake of 1906 made a lasting impression on eight-year-old Dorothy.
Courtesy of Marquette University Archives

Dorothy (center) with her sister, Della, and a cousin.
Throughout her life Dorothy remained especially
close to Della and her younger brother, John.
Courtesy of Marquette University Archives

Dorothy left home to attend the University of Illinois when she was just sixteen. Joining the Scribblers' Club at the university (pictured here in 1915; Dorothy is in the center, back row) gave Dorothy a chance to make friends and develop her talent for writing.

Dorothy left the University of Illinois in the spring of 1916. Several months later, she (in the middle, above) got her first job working for the New York *Call*, a Socialist newspaper that opposed U.S. entry into World War I.

Dorothy was a human whirlwind for the next several years. Among
other things, she wrote for several papers, worked as a nurse, was
married briefly, lived on the island of Capri, and wrote a novel.
When a publisher gave her $5,000 for the manuscript, she bought
a small cottage on Staten Island, where this picture was taken
(about 1925). During the few years that she lived here,
she had a loving but difficult relationship with
Forster Batterham and gave birth to her daughter, Tamar.

After Dorothy left Staten
Island in 1927, she moved
from place to place for
several years, supporting
herself and Tamar with a
variety of jobs. Shortly after
she returned to New York
City in 1932, she met Peter
Maurin, and the Catholic
Worker movement was
born. Here are the first
headquarters on East
Fifteenth Street.
Courtesy of
Marquette University Archives

Dorothy (at the far right)
in the office of the first headquarters in the fall of 1934.
Photo by Henry Beck; courtesy of Marquette University Archives

During the 1930s, the Catholic Worker movement — forever
growing — moved its headquarters from Fifteenth Street to
Charles Street to Mott Street. Here, at the Mott Street
location, a familiar sight: the daily breadline.
Courtesy of Marquette University Archives

The Catholic Worker movement spawned "houses of hospitality"
across the country. Here Dorothy (second from right) visits the
Holy Family House of the Milwaukee Catholic Worker Community.
Photo by Michael Strasser; courtesy of Marquette University Archives

Dorothy and Tamar, about 1932. Although her commitment to the
Catholic Worker movement took a great deal of time and energy,
Dorothy remained very close and devoted to Tamar.

CATHOLIC WORKER

Vol. XLI. No. 4   MAY, 1975   Subscription 25c Per Year   Price 1¢

Lord, Make Us Instruments of Your Peace

Poverty

The following article is reprinted from the September, 1950 Catholic Worker. William Gauchat was the founder of Blessed Martin House in Cleveland in the early days of the Catholic Worker Movement. With his wife, Dorothy, he co-founded Our Lady of the Wayside Home for handicapped children. We reprint this article in gratitude for his life. Eds. note.)

By WILLIAM GAUCHAT

> What a fine place
> this world would be
> if Roman Catholics
> tried to keep up
> with St. Francis of Assisi."
> (Peter Maurin)

Hilaire Belloc begins one of his essays with whimsical irony by relating how he started a speech in this wise: POVERTY

1 The attainment of it.

2 The retention of it when attained. It appears that no one was interested and and he was addressing a vacant hall.

The reaction seems to be different when a Catholic Worker speaks of the need for **voluntary poverty.** Those two words are like dynamite to wake up a sleeping person usually too timid to acknowledge the time of day will protest in deep tones of indignation. There is nothing dull in the discussion then, neither is there any clarity. It is my purpose here, with the grace of God, in the quiet of the farmhouse with all the children in bed, I try to define what voluntary poverty means to me. Why I feel it is the shortest cut to a full and happy life.

David said: "Blessed is he that understands concerning the poor."

Christ said: "The poor you have always with you."

St. Francis loved poverty, and with the courtesy of a troubadour regarded Lady Poverty as his lovely mistress. And Leon Bloy, who lived a long life with her, speaks thus: "The angels are silent, and the trembling Devils tear out their tongues rather than speak. Only the idiots of our own generation have taken upon themselves to elucidate this mystery. Meanwhile, till the deep shall swallow them up, Poverty walks tranquilly in her mask, bearing her sieve."

At the beginning it must be insisted of underlined, Poverty is not pauper

ON PILGRIMAGE

By DOROTHY DAY

When we were growing up, we were taught that it was in bad taste to talk about money, and yet one finds Anthony Trollope's and Jane Austen's characters constantly talking about income. "Aunt Greenow has a fortune of 40,000 pounds" changes that had to be made, fire-retarding stairs, steel self-closing doors new bathrooms on each floor, etc., etc. Plans were submitted for approval to holy mother the City. Architects, contractors, plumbers, professional men all ... and finally these blueprints, so were approved. ..., $110,000 up to ired to make a ... who had been

Nonviolence

By EILEEN EGAN

Nonviolence has a negative, passive ring to it that its adherents have been attempting to erase by prefixing to it the adjective "militant." Regrettably, it is the only current term in general usage in English. It corresponds to the Gandhian "ahimsa," non-injury, and does carry the necessary message of unwillingness to injure or kill other creatures. For Western adherents of "ahimsa" or nonviolence, who are not vegetarians, the unwillingness applies only to human creatures. The nonviolent person is not supine before an insane attack. The defense of a third party often involves the interposing of the body of the nonviolent person, with no intent of inflicting harm.

Gandhi coined the term "satyagraha," truth-force, to describe a nonviolent campaign for human rights and freedom. As "God is Truth and Truth is God" in Gandhi's thinking, the inference was that only godly or moral force would be employed by "satyagrahi," participants in the nonviolent movement. Martin Luther King's term, "soul-force" is a satisfactory one for most adherents of nonviolence.

A commitment to nonviolence as a way of life and of achieving change has deep implications for personal life and personal relationships, for community and social actions, and for the conduct of the nation.

A striking example of the implications of the acceptance of nonviolence for one's personal life is narrated in **The Book of Ammon**, autobiography of Ammon Hennacy. In July 1917, as a 24 year-old prisoner, Ammon arrived at Atlanta Federal Penitentiary to serve a two-year sentence for anti-draft activity. This was separate from a sentence, to be served later, for his own refusal to register for the draft. Ammon, prisoner 7438, was not long in Atlanta when he stirred up activity. He led his fellow-prisoners in a mass refusal to appear at the mess hall as a protest against rotten food.

For this action, Ammon was condemned to solitary confinement. Though his teeth began to ache, he could not persuade the warden to allow him to see a dentist. Ammon wrote that, in his heart, he longed for a weapon and "mentally tallied those whom I desired to kill when I was free."

Ammon was allowed a bible and it became his only companion. In "the hole" He read the New Testament many times and recalled that he went over the Sermon on the Mount scores of times. He

Dorothy at
Maryfarm in Easton,
Pennsylvania, about
1937. The Catholic
Workers' first farm
provided Dorothy
with times of both
delight and
disappointment.
Courtesy of Marquette
University Archives

A group picture taken at Maryfarm in Easton, about 1945.
Dorothy is third from the left in the back row;
Peter Maurin is sixth from the left.
Courtesy of Marquette University Archives

Dorothy and Peter Maurin in 1948 at the "second" Maryfarm,
located in Newburgh, New York. This property served
as both a farm and a retreat center.
Courtesy of Marquette University Archives

After Peter Maurin's death in 1949, the Catholic Worker purchased
a piece of property on Staten Island and called it Peter Maurin
Farm. This photo gives a rear view of the buildings.
Photo by William Carter

Ammon Hennacy (in February 1955), who joined the
Catholic Worker movement in 1952.
He was ardent about pacifism — and about Dorothy.
Photo by Vivian Cherry; courtesy of Marquette University Archives

Dorothy and Ammon
Hennacy during one of the
many protests against
civil-defense drills in New
York City. Their mutual
admiration and shared
commitments didn't lead to
romance, but they were the
basis of a long friendship.
Photo by Mottke Weissman;
courtesy of Marquette University
Archives

During one of the civil-defense drills in 1956,
Dorothy, Ammon Hennacy, and others staged a
sit-down protest in Washington Square Park.
Photo by Robert Lax; courtesy of Marquette University Archives

Life was more than protests and picket lines. Dorothy (shown here
with Ammon) always set aside time for Tamar and her children.
Photo taken in the late fifties; supplied courtesy of Marquette University Archives

The sixties were another decade of protest. On November 6, 1965, Dorothy met with A.J. Muste in Union Square at a draft card burning protest. Muste has been called "the dean of American pacifists."
Courtesy of Tom Cornell

Dorothy continued to picket in the seventies, when *she* was in her seventies. Here she sits on a picket line in Lamont, California, talking with a nun and others as police stand by. Later, Dorothy was among the 300 people arrested.
Photo by Bob Fitch; courtesy of Catholic News Service

Dorothy with Coretta Scott King at a service for farmworkers
at the Episcopal Cathedral of St. John the Divine in
New York, where Cesar Chavez was holding a rally
in support of California farmworkers.
Courtesy of Catholic News Service

Dorothy and Mother Teresa having tea in June 1979 at Maryhouse,
the Catholic Worker's shelter for homeless women in New York
City, where Dorothy spent most of her final years.
(Dorothy died on November 29, 1980, at the age of eighty-three.)
Photo by Bill Barrett

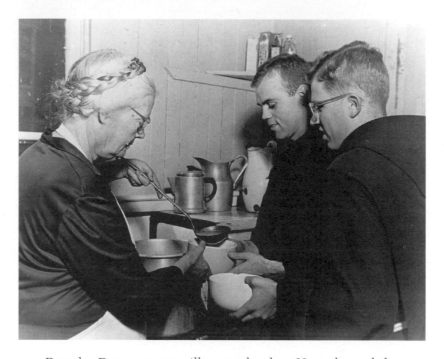

Dorothy Day as many will remember her. Here she and the
Franciscan seminarians from Duns Scotus College work in the
serving line at St. Francis House in Detroit. What her friend
Daniel Berrigan wrote about her serves as a fitting remembrance:
"The simple task, the one practically everyone boggled at
or bowed out of, this she would do."

Dorothy was less than enthusiastic about the plan. She had lived in cities most of her life, and she felt that New York was home. She was so busy with the paper and the house of hospitality that she could hardly imagine starting another new venture. But the young Catholic Workers around her were caught up in Peter's excitement. Night after night, they sat in the kitchen making plans.

Peter wanted the first farming commune to have at least twelve acres, but the Catholic Workers couldn't afford such a large piece of land. At last they rented a small one-acre farm near Huguenot on Staten Island. This choice fueled Dorothy's enthusiasm for Peter's plan. Dorothy had loved Staten Island ever since she had lived there with Forster Batterham. The farm was close to the Catholic boarding school that Tamar attended and was within an easy journey of the city. Dorothy had always treasured her peaceful rides back and forth on the Staten Island ferry. Now she would be taking the ferry again.

Late in the spring of 1935, a small, eager group of Catholic Workers moved to the farm near Huguenot. It was so small that they nicknamed it the "garden commune." Still, they hoped that their experience would lay a foundation for the real farm they would have some day. The garden commune would set an example. Looking back, Dorothy wrote ironically that "the kinds of people who were attracted to our garden commune . . . without doubt, were the last people in the world capable of making a foundation, setting an example, or leading a way."

Peter distrusted authority on any terms. He believed that, given an opportunity, each individual would make his or her best contribution to the community. Consequently, no one was officially in charge at the garden commune. No one gave orders. Everyone was simply expected to pitch in and do his or her share of the work.

Not surprisingly, problems were often the consequence of good intentions. One of the workers who came to live on the farm was a former drug addict who spent most of his time trying to devise a universal language. He felt he contributed to the community by gathering driftwood and other fuel on the beach. Sometimes he would stuff the furnace with damp wood, old shoes, and other debris he had collected, and accidentally put out the fire in the process. A group of college students decided to make pottery with clay they dug up along the shore. Whenever they washed their hands and their tools in the kitchen sink, they clogged up the drain.

Priests and nuns sent people newly released from psychiatric hospitals, many of them too disturbed to take real responsibility. But one man, though obviously psychotic, proved an invaluable member of the community. His name was Edelson, and he was a Jewish immigrant from Eastern Europe. Day after day he worked barefoot in the garden. Sometimes he slid his toes slowly through the dirt, as if he were caressing the earth. When the first shoots sprouted, he looked at them lovingly and exclaimed, "I drew them up out the ground with the power of my eyes!" He often said that he gave his labor to the garden commune "for the sake of communism, a Holy Communism, comradeship, cooperation, brotherhood, unity." "Christ was in his heart," Dorothy wrote. "We loved him."

Sadly, not everyone at the farm appreciated Edelson's presence. One day at lunch Edelson picked up a piece of black bread, held it in the air, and announced, "I am Lenin, and these are my words: this is my body broken for you." Convinced that Edelson was a madman, one of the scholars staying at the farm threatened to have him locked up in an institution. Edelson left that day and was never seen again.

All summer, conflicts erupted between the "workers" and the "scholars." Workers like Steve Hergenhan, a German carpenter, put in endless hours hoeing the fields and repairing the house. The scholars, on the other hand, were inclined to spend their time in the shade on the wide wooden porch, debating issues like freedom versus authority and charity versus justice. Resentments smoldered and flared and smoldered again. But somehow vegetables grew, and there were fresh tomatoes and green beans for the community back on Mott Street.

Despite the tensions at Huguenot, the Workers were eager to move to a real farm. In the fall of 1935, Dorothy received a letter from a retired teacher in Baltimore, a *Catholic Worker* subscriber. The teacher promised the group a thousand dollars toward the purchase of a farm. Her only condition was that the Workers should give her three acres of the farm they purchased and build her a house where she could live for the rest of her life. In this way, she explained, she would put some of the unemployed men to work and not merely give them handouts.

Dorothy was dismayed by the scolding tone of the letter. She wrote back that the Workers were "a rather slipshod group of individuals who were trying to work out certain principles — the chief of which was an analysis of man's freedom and what it implied." She warned that they could not put people out into the street, even if they acted irrationally and hatefully. The Workers were trying to overcome hatred with love, to change troubled people "from lions into lambs. It was a practice in loving, a learning to love, a paying of the cost of love."

But the Baltimore teacher was not discouraged by Dorothy's response, and so the plan proceeded. That winter, Dorothy and several of the Workers visited farms all over Pennsylvania and New Jersey. At last, in April, they found the place they wanted, a sprawling twenty-eight acres outside Easton, Pennsylvania. Big Dan, the driver for the group that day, threw himself on the grass and exclaimed, "Back to the land!" Dorothy later wrote, "It was a climb up to the barn, a race down to the spring, and a climb back up to the pasture." The place cost $1,250; the Catholic Workers put in an offer on the spot. Jubilant, they returned to Mott Street with fresh eggs, dandelion greens, and dreams of the good life that was about to begin.

Maryfarm, as they named the new farming commune, was not quite as perfect as the Workers had first imagined. The biggest problem was a lack of water; the spring that the Workers had raced down to proved to be on their neighbor's property. Eventually they were able to dig a well, but at first they made do with cisterns that collected rainwater. Money problems continued to plague the group; there was never quite enough to buy all of the things they needed. One college student who spent a summer at the farm recalled that he lived chiefly on lettuce.

Every summer, children from the slums of Harlem came out to spend time at the farm. Free from her boarding school, Tamar joined them in exploring the woods and playing with the kittens and baby pigs. Many people came who were in need of care because of physical or mental illness. Frank, recently released from Sing Sing Prison, planted roses and petunias. One guest had worked as a strong man with the circus, doing an act in which a troupe of Russian acrobats made a human pyramid on his shoulders. When the moon was full, he liked to turn cartwheels down the hill behind the house.

Several men who had been involved in the seamen's strike joined the Maryfarm community and tried their hand at raising potatoes and asparagus. One, John Filligar, stayed for several years. During his first visit he was painting the barn when he slipped from his ladder and plunged about forty feet. He survived the accident with no major injuries because he landed in a soft pile of manure. John saw the incident as a sign from God that he was meant to remain at the farm.

Considering what a diverse community the Workers had created, people got along surprisingly well. And Maryfarm could provide moments of pure delight. In December of 1936, Dorothy gave this report in *The Catholic Worker*:

> The happiest and most joyful event of the month was the birth of a calf on the Catholic Worker farm. At three o'clock in the afternoon Victor left his pots and pans to go up to the barn cistern for water and looked in to say hello to the cow. She was placidly munching then. An hour later Jim and John Filligar went in, and there was the calf. I got down to the farm three hours later and the little one was gamboling around, answering to the name of Bess, and actually cavorting with the joy of life that was in her. . . . We were all so happy, and it was one of those moments of pure unalloyed joy so rare in this life.

Nevertheless, a certain amount of bickering and dissatisfaction was inevitable. Whenever Dorothy arrived at Maryfarm, she faced a long series of grievances. In one essay she described the discouragement she sometimes felt:

"Are we trying to make a farm here, or aren't we?" A statement of that kind, an attitude of criticism of all that Peter and I stand for, has the power to down me completely. . . . Nothing but the grace of God can help me, but I feel utterly lacking, ineffective. . . . I have had this completely alone feeling. A temptation of the devil, doubtless, and to succumb to it is a lack of faith and hope. There is nothing to do but bear it, but my heart is as heavy as lead, and my mind dull and uninspired. A time when the memory and understanding fail one completely and only the will remains, so that I feel hard and rigid, and at the same time ready to sit like a soft fool and weep.

The practical concerns of farm life could seem overwhelming. But Dorothy made sure that the group never lost its Christian focus. In 1939, the Maryfarm community spent three days in its first religious retreat. It was a time of silence, contemplation, and prayer that Dorothy hoped would bring them all closer to God. "For three days we had a closed retreat, silence was kept, as much as was humanly possible, no problems were discussed, no reading was done which was not spiritual," Dorothy wrote in *The Catholic Worker*. "It was a time of real happiness. . . . By the time this retreat was over, and we gathered together for a social evening of talk and discussion, we found such unity amongst us all, that there seemed no reason for discussion. When we separated, it was with pain, we hated to leave each other, we loved each other more truly than before, and felt that sense of comradeship, that sense of Christian solidarity which will strengthen us for the work."

By joining together in this spirit of Christian love, the Catholic Workers became a community in the deepest, truest sense.

CHAPTER 9

The Troubled Path of Peace

"Tonight I have to speak, and I am so fatigued by a two-week speaking trip that I am miserable about it," wrote Dorothy in her journal in May of 1937. "It is only with the greatest effort that I speak. The idea depresses me for a day beforehand. I get physically sick from it."

From the first days of *The Catholic Worker,* people all over the United States invited Dorothy Day to give public lectures. As she indicated in her journal, she was painfully shy when she had to address a roomful of strangers. Nevertheless, she knew that her talks helped spread the personalist philosophy of the Catholic Worker movement, the message that each individual must serve humanity through his or her actions, performed in the spirit of Christian love. She spoke to high school and college students, to women's clubs, to church groups, and to conventions of doctors and social workers. Clearly and directly, without looking at notes, she explained that all people belonged to "the Body of Christ." By helping those in need, she told her audiences, they were actually helping Christ himself.

Some of the Catholic Workers resented Dorothy's frequent absences. Whenever she was away, a crisis seemed to erupt at Mott Street or at Maryfarm. Besides, some complained, why should Dorothy escape the squalor and strife of the house of hospitality, while others had to stay behind and serve on the breadline?

Yet no one could argue with the fact that Dorothy's lectures brought in desperately needed funds. She didn't charge a speaker's fee, but she gratefully accepted any donations people offered after hearing her talks. She channeled most of this money back into the newspaper and other Catholic Worker programs. In addition, Dorothy's talks inspired the founding of new houses of hospitality and farming communes across the country. The Catholic Worker movement was gaining momentum.

From Philadelphia to Oklahoma City, on across the Great Plains to California, then east again to Chicago, Detroit, and Buffalo — Dorothy Day crisscrossed the nation by bus and by train. Though she often found travel exhausting, the long rides gave her much-needed privacy. On a train to San Francisco she wrote in her journal, "These hours on the train or bus are so precious! To be alone for a short while! It is a complete relaxation, a joy. I am a weak and faulty vessel to be freighted with so valuable a message as cargo."

Like Dorothy, Peter Maurin was frequently asked to give talks. Without hesitation, Peter would go anywhere and talk to anyone who might listen. His sole purpose in life was to convey his ideas about building a better society. Yet Peter hardly looked the part of a dignified public speaker. He had no interest at all in his personal appearance. When he traveled, he would go for days without bathing or changing his clothes. In cold weather he slept in bus stations; in the summer he preferred to sleep by the side of a road, folding his pants beneath his head as a pillow.

Once Peter was invited to speak to a group of women in an affluent town north of New York City. Several hours after she took him to the train station, Dorothy received a frantic phone call. Peter Maurin had never arrived. Dorothy told the caller that Peter must be at the train station, and she urged the woman to look around. "But there's no one here," the caller insisted, "only an old tramp sitting on a bench." Dorothy assured her that the "old tramp" was the lecturer she was waiting to meet. Another time, Peter was invited to dinner at the home of a distinguished university professor. When he arrived, the professor's wife thought he had come to read the gas meter, and so she sent him to the basement. There he sat patiently for several hours, until the professor realized what had happened.

Busy though she always was, Dorothy managed to find time for her family. She remained especially close to her sister, Della, and to her younger brother, John, and his wife. She saw less of her brother Donald, though their relationship was cordial. Her brother Sam, however, was deeply conservative and regarded her with suspicion. Relations between them were cool throughout her life.

Dorothy was very close to her mother and visited her as often as she could. By the late 1930s, her parents had moved to Florida, where her father helped to found the Hialeah Racetrack. Atheist that he was, Dorothy's father was appalled by the direction her life had taken. In 1937 he wrote to a relative, "Dorothy, the oldest girl, is the nut of the family. When she came out of the university she was a Communist. Now she's a Catholic crusader. She runs a Catholic paper, and skyhoots all over the country delivering lectures. . . . She was in Miami last winter and lived out with [cousins] Clem and Kate. I wouldn't have her around me." Her father died two years later, never having reconciled with Dorothy. Yet Dorothy recalled her father with tenderness. She saw him as a man who loved beauty, the beauty he saw in the grace and speed of running horses.

In 1938, Dorothy Day told the story of her conversion to Catholicism in a book entitled *From Union Square to Rome*. In another book, *House of Hospitality* (1939), she described life at the house on Mott Street. Like her lectures, the books spread the Catholic Worker's message across the land.

But the popularity of that message did not remain constant. Through its first three years of publication, *The*

Catholic Worker won high praise from churchmen and lay readers alike. Like Dorothy herself, many Catholics were eager for a way to battle the world's social ills from within a Christian framework. Before the Catholic Worker movement had been launched, only the Communists had seemed to offer hope to the destitute. Now Dorothy Day provided a means to win back the poor from Communism to a community of Christian fellowship.

But in 1936, public opinion toward the Catholic Worker movement shifted. A bloody civil war had erupted in faraway Spain. American radicals supported the Spanish Communists. Most Catholics, on the other hand, backed General Francisco Franco, who promised to defeat the Communists and keep the Catholic Church alive. Dorothy Day and *The Catholic Worker* refused to champion either side. Instead, the paper took a firm pacifist stand, totally rejecting war as a solution to human problems. Looking back to her Socialist past, Dorothy saw war as the devastating end result of capitalism, with bankers and bosses fighting to protect their investments. As a Catholic, she felt that war was completely contrary to Christ's teachings about brotherhood and forgiveness. The taking of human life, in any form and for any reason, was the willful destruction of God's creation.

Most Roman Catholics were shocked and appalled by the paper's stance. Surely, they argued, a war against Godless Communists was justified. But *The Catholic Worker* insisted that there could be no just wars. All warfare, under any circumstances, was evil.

In the furor over the Spanish Civil War, *The Catholic Worker* lost many loyal subscribers. But the trouble had only begun. In Germany, soldiers were marching under the banner of a dynamic new leader named Adolf Hitler. The world was preparing for a war of destruction on a scale never before imagined. The United States opened new weapons plants, getting ready for the conflict ahead. "We oppose preparedness for war," Dorothy wrote in *The Catholic Worker.* "[Preparedness] will undoubtedly lead to war." In an editorial she wrote, "As long as men trust to the use of force, only a more savage and brutal force will overcome the enemy. We use his own weapons, and we must make sure our own force is more savage and more bestial than his own. If we do not emphasize the law of love, we betray our trust, our vocation." Following Christ's example, one must meet violence with love. One must reject war, even if it meant suffering and death.

On December 7, 1941, Japanese planes bombed the American fleet at Pearl Harbor in Hawaii. In response, the United States plunged into war with Japan, and then with Germany. Fiery speeches and news of the enemy's atrocities whipped the nation into a frenzy of patriotic zeal. Long-silent factories reopened and poured out rifles, ammunition, tanks, and uniforms. The Great Depression was over at last. Suddenly there were jobs for nearly everyone.

As more and more men and women found work in war plants, the breadline at Mott Street dwindled. Many of the young people who were part of the Catholic Worker community couldn't accept pacifism at this time of national crisis. Each month, more of the young men volunteered or were drafted into the armed forces. Both men and women took jobs in defense plants.

Dorothy grieved that so many Catholic Workers abandoned the movement's pacifist principles. Even those who stood with her were often obliged to leave the Worker community. Young men who refused to fight on religious grounds could be excused from military service and officially declared "conscientious objectors." But they were then obliged to spend several years performing government-mandated service in hospitals or psychiatric institutions. The Catholic Church didn't encourage its members to oppose war. But several of the Catholic Workers served as conscientious objectors during World War II.

With fewer and fewer hands to cook meals and care for the guests, Dorothy relied heavily on David Mason. David was a quiet, slow-moving man of forty-five who spent his spare time trying to invent a machine that could type Chinese characters. One day, two FBI agents appeared at the Mott Street house and announced that they had come for David. They found him in the kitchen, busy preparing gelatin for supper, and placed him under arrest because he had failed to register for the draft. To the dismay of everyone in the house, David was taken to a detention center, still protesting that the gelatin was not done. Fortunately, the charges against him were dropped because of his age, and he was back at Mott Street within a week.

During the war, thousands of people canceled their subscriptions to *The Catholic Worker,* unable to accept its pacifist stand. In Milwaukee, in Philadelphia, in cities all across the country, houses of hospitality were forced to close their doors. In addition, Dorothy's unshakeable position cut her off from some of her closest friends. The director of one house of hospitality decided to leave the Catholic Worker movement altogether, and wrote to Dorothy sadly, "Something I had, and others too, I guess, is gone forever. Damn war! Damn Pacifism and stands! . . . One of the saddest parts of the whole business is the knowledge that there is no coming back — it is all over — to the warmth and understanding we once knew together. Profound disagreement is a wall between people and it rears higher every day. How I wish you weren't a heretic! And sometimes how I wish that I were one too. But to agree with you means cutting myself off from a much larger world and that pain is one you must know well, so that my anguish of separation is meager in comparison."

The war years placed Dorothy under severe strain. Sometimes the tension brought on terrible headaches and backaches. While friends and strangers alike accused her of being unpatriotic, the usual wrangling continued at Mott Street and Maryfarm. Guests complained constantly and made impossible demands. Dorothy had no peace.

Some of the people who came to Mott Street were potentially violent. One man had spent years in a psychiatric hospital after he tried to kill his brother. Another guest, Michael, had been dismissed from a seminary because of his mental illness. He insisted that Dorothy should get him re-admitted to the program. In her journal she wrote that he "would come in and stand over me, and with livid face . . . call down curses from heaven upon me, damning my soul to the lowest hell for interfering, as he said, with his vocation. He was going to see to it, he protested, that I was going to be punished, and all who worked with me. . . . I was afraid, coming and going."

As if these worries weren't enough, Dorothy spent the war years preoccupied with Tamar and Tamar's future. Tamar was a bright girl who enjoyed reading, but she didn't care for school. She was happiest at Maryfarm, tending to the animals. She had little interest in going to college. One day, in a moment of frustration, Tamar exclaimed that she wished she were mentally retarded. Then she wouldn't be expected to study history and mathematics and foreign languages. She could attend a vocational program and learn useful things — how to cook and sew and budget for a household.

Through a friend who was a priest, Dorothy learned of a unique boarding-school for girls outside Montreal in Canada. There Tamar could learn to use a spinning wheel, to weave cloth, to sew, and to cook. Tamar was delighted, but Dorothy found it hard to send her daughter so far away. Tamar spent a semester at the school, and mother and daughter exchanged postcards nearly every day. Dorothy also found it difficult to accept Tamar's desire to marry young — that would mean a more fundamental separation between them. Dorothy described her feelings vividly in her autobiography: "When I left Tamar that afternoon . . ., I never was so unhappy, never felt so great a sense of loneliness. She was growing up, she was growing up to be married. It did not seem possible. I was always having to be parted from her. No matter how many times I gave up mother, father, husband, brother, daughter, for His sake, I had to do it over again."

In 1942, the summer she was sixteen, Tamar returned to Maryfarm. There she met David Hennessy, a young man who had recently joined the farming commune. Dorothy soon realized that the two had fallen in love. She tried to discourage the relationship, convinced that Tamar was too young to think about marriage. But by the end of the summer, Tamar and David had made up their minds. At last Dorothy agreed that Tamar could get married as soon as she turned eighteen.

In the summer of 1943, Dorothy Day made a decision that amazed and dismayed the people around her. She needed a rest, she explained, and she wanted to spend time with Tamar before her wedding. More than anything else, she needed time to be alone, peace for contemplation and prayer. For a year she was going to leave the Catholic Worker. "The world is too much with me," she wrote in one of her notebooks. "The world is suffering and dying. I am not suffering and dying in the Catholic Worker. I am writing and talking about it. Of course I will not save my soul alone. Wherever we are we are with people. We drag them down or pull them up. Or we get dragged down or pulled up. And in recognition of this latter fact, I recognize also the need for aids and counsels in the path to God. That is why as soon as possible I will try to organize days of recollection — primarily for myself. I will not be able to stand the impact of the world otherwise."

Dorothy spent the next several months on Long Island, where Tamar was taking classes at a junior college in Farmingdale. Seldom had she and her daughter found so much time to enjoy each other's company. Dorothy also spent many happy hours with her mother, who was now widowed and ill and living in nearby Mineola. (After her mother's death in 1945, Dorothy was especially glad that they had been able to have this rich and rewarding time together.)

Dorothy spent much of her time in solitary retreat at a convent of the Dominican Sisters near Farmingdale. She attended Mass, prayed, and read the Bible and other books that she loved for their power to inspire her. Gradually she felt that her strength and energy were restored.

Shortly after her period of retreat was over, Dorothy wrote about the experience in one of her notebooks:

I got up at 6:30 for a seven o'clock Mass. . . . Then

after a solitary breakfast, the only meal I enjoyed during the day, I returned to the chapel for another two hours of praying and meditative reading. . . . The litanies, the rosary, repetitive prayer always helped to put me in an attitude of adoration and thanksgiving and petition. Sometimes I prayed with joy and delight. Other times each bead of my rosary was heavy as lead. My steps dragged, my lips were numb. I felt a dead weight. I could do nothing but make an act of will and sit or kneel, and sigh in an agony of boredom. Taking refuge in St. Benedict's advice to pray often and in short prayers I took flight on these occasions and walked, or went back to my room and read or tried to work. . . .

In the afternoon I tried to rest but restlessness was often my portion. I read also two hours daily on Goodier's *Life of Christ,* which I have found unequalled. . . .

I came to the conclusion during those months that such a hermit's life for a woman was impossible. Man is not meant to live alone. To cook for one's self, to eat by one's self, to sew, wash, clean for one's self is a sterile joy. Community, whether of the family, or convent, or boarding house, is absolutely necessary.

Inevitably, that need for community drew Dorothy back to the Catholic Worker. She returned to Mott Street in the spring of 1944. Except for her speaking tours and brief travels with friends, she remained with the Catholic Worker for the rest of her life.

In April of 1944, Tamar and David were married in

the parish church near Maryfarm. Dorothy rose at dawn to make preparations for the wedding breakfast so that it could be served after the early-morning ceremony. Peter Maurin hovered about the kitchen, expounding on communal sharing versus the profit motive. Tamar whispered that she hoped Peter wouldn't make a speech to her wedding guests. As discreetly as she could, Dorothy tried to explain to Peter that this was a very special day in Tamar's life, that she did not want to think just now about philosophical issues.

After the ceremony, the wedding party of neighbors and priests, Catholic Workers and guests from Mott Street returned to the farmhouse. The breakfast was ready — ham and fresh eggs served with endless cups of steaming coffee. Everyone was in high spirits. Tamar kept running outside to check on two orphaned baby goats that she was feeding from a bottle. "And then," Dorothy recalled in her autobiography, "Peter began his speech! We all laughed, but we all had to listen too. After all, it would not have been a Catholic Worker wedding without it. . . . It was an occasion, and occasions called for speeches. And speeches were always affairs of moment with Peter. There were no idle words with him. When he spoke, it was 'yea, yea' or 'nay, nay.' But it took him a long time to say it."

In September of 1945, banner headlines across the nation shouted the news of victory: the war was over. Bands played and cheering crowds filled the streets. But

107

in *The Catholic Worker,* a somber headline told of world leaders signing papers upon the ruins of defeated nations. A terrible new weapon, the atomic bomb, had brought unimaginable destruction to the Japanese cities of Hiroshima and Nagasaki. Surely this was no time for rejoicing. The war was over at last, but what lessons had been learned?

CHAPTER 10

The End of an Era

By the end of the war, Maryfarm had ceased to be productive. Too many people came and went, wrestling over authority like puppies fighting for a bone. In 1944, the Catholic Worker closed the Easton property as a working farm and opened it as a retreat center. Several times a year, groups of priests, nuns, and lay people were invited to the farm for a form of spiritual refreshment that Dorothy found more and more necessary to her own life. But after a few years, when a contentious family took over the upper farmhouse and created a kind of permanent conflict there, Maryfarm was closed. Shortly thereafter, in 1947, the Catholic Worker purchased property at Newburgh, New York, which served as both a farm (though not a profitable one) and a center for retreats. This new retreat center was also called Maryfarm.

"The beauty of the young people gathered together on a retreat!" Dorothy wrote ecstatically after one weekend.

"We wander between hedges of wild cherry making the stations [of the Cross], or under the great and ancient oaks, or sit under the maples and the pines watching the traffic, which has all the fascination and movement of flowing streams. . . . There is the beauty of all the seasons on this land, on these farms which have been made beautiful and fruitful by hard work, the hard work of saints and sinners and all the in-betweens."

Dorothy realized that she needed these retreats just as much as the others who gathered at Maryfarm: "It is not only for others that I must have these retreats. It is because I too am hungry and thirsty for the bread of the strong. I too must nourish myself to do the work I have undertaken; I too must drink these good springs so that I may not be an empty cistern and unable to help others."

An ongoing source of anxiety for Dorothy was Tamar. In the years after Tamar's marriage to David Hennessy, Dorothy was constantly worried about the young couple. Their attempts at farming seemed doomed to failure. For four years they lived on a farm in northern Virginia, in a house without running water or central heating. Every year, it seemed, Tamar had a new baby. Caring for her small children left her constantly exhausted, and she wrote to her mother that she felt a deep loneliness. This prompted Dorothy to reflect again on loneliness and the human condition: "The only answer in this life, to the loneliness we are all bound to feel, is community. The living together, working together, sharing together, loving God and loving our brother, and living close to him in community so that we can show our love for Him."

To try to ease Tamar's discomfort, Dorothy visited when she could, and she sent money she earned by selling articles to newspapers and magazines. When her worries overwhelmed her, she would reflect that she had turned away from God and lost herself in human concerns. Then she would call herself back and find comfort in prayer.

The speech that Peter Maurin gave at Tamar's wedding breakfast was one of the last he ever delivered. A few months later he had a stroke in his sleep, from which he never fully recovered. Over the next five years he grew steadily weaker and more confused. At last he had to be bathed and dressed like a small child, and watched constantly to make certain he didn't wander outside and get lost. As long as he was able to walk, he managed to attend Mass every day.

During the final two years of his life, Peter Maurin lived at the farm in Newburgh, surrounded by loving friends. Sometimes he sat in the kitchen, straining to follow whatever debate was underway. But, as he exclaimed in anguish, "I can no longer think." The man who had devoted his life to "clarification of thought" through discussion could find nothing more to say.

In her autobiography, Dorothy explained, "If he had been a babbler, he would have been a babbler to the end. But when he could no longer think, as he himself expressed it, he remained silent." Peter had lived a life of true voluntary poverty. He owned almost nothing beyond a few books. For most of his years with the Catholic Worker, he had not even had a bed of his own, but had slept wherever there was room at the house of hospitality. Now, Dorothy reflected, "He had stripped himself, but there remained work for God to do. We are to be pruned as the vine is pruned so that it can bear fruit, and this we cannot do ourselves. God did it for him. He took from him his mind, the one thing he had left, the one thing perhaps he took delight in." In the end, Peter was at peace. He felt he had completed the work he set out to do. The rest would be carried forward by a new generation.

Peter died quietly in the house at Newburgh on June 15, 1949. The following day his body was moved to Mott Street and laid out in the storefront room that usually served as the newspaper office. All day long, neighbors and friends, priests and derelicts, factory workers and philosophers filed past the coffin to pay their last respects. Some touched their rosaries to Peter's folded hands or bent to kiss his cold, gray cheek. More than ever before, Dorothy was convinced that Peter Maurin had been a saint.

Peter's death marked the end of an era in Dorothy Day's life. For seventeen years she had listened to his lectures, studied his essays, lived with his eccentricities, and worked to put his ideas into practice. Now, at the age of seventy-two, Peter was gone. His legacy, the

Catholic Worker movement, would carry on without him.

Dorothy herself was beginning to feel the weight of the years upon her. At fifty-two she found herself gasping for breath as she climbed to her tiny fifth-floor room in the house on Mott Street. The house oppressed her with its noise, dirt, and cockroaches. She cherished her quiet times — her Catholic Worker retreats and the days she spent with Tamar and the children. When the Catholic Worker purchased a piece of property on Staten Island, to be called Peter Maurin Farm, she enjoyed once again the peaceful ferry ride back and forth from Manhattan.

In the spring of 1950, Dorothy learned that the house on Mott Street, which had been put on the market by the woman who owned it, had been sold. The house had served the Catholic Worker for the past fourteen years. Now, within three months, the whole community would have to move.

As she had done countless times before, Dorothy Day turned to the readers of *The Catholic Worker* for help. Her appeal in the paper, combined with personal pleas to friends of the movement all over the country, brought in the needed money by early June. And Dorothy felt that prayer had a great deal to do with it too: "I know that we all prayed, coming and going, night and day, sleeping and waking." So the Catholic Worker was able to purchase a large house at 223 Chrystie Street, a block from the Bowery (Manhattan's famous "Skid Row"), and move in that summer. The new house of hospitality had a large front yard, a wide, elegant porch, and, best of all, hot running water! The Catholic Workers bid a glad farewell to the cold showers of their voluntary poverty.

During World War II, the federal government had seemed to have little concern with the pacifism of the Catholic Worker movement. The voices of Dorothy Day and her followers had been like whispers in a gale, protesting in vain against a war that had gotten overwhelming public support. In the early 1950s, however, the nation was swept by uncertainty and fear. The Soviet Union had emerged as a threatening world power, and many Americans worried that Communism could engulf the globe. Senator Joseph McCarthy of Wisconsin fanned these fears into a frenzy. He warned that Communists were everywhere — in the schools, in Hollywood, in the halls of government. The FBI launched a nationwide investigation to search out the enemy.

With her past Communist sympathies and her ongoing protests against the military, Dorothy Day was an obvious suspect. In fact, nearly everyone connected with the Catholic Worker movement came under government scrutiny. For a time, FBI agents visited the house on Chrystie Street almost daily, questioning and probing. Some of the Workers took the situation lightly, but others lived in constant fear of arrest.

Dorothy remained untroubled by the intrusion. On one occasion, an FBI agent arrived to question her about one of the Workers, a conscientious objector. "He asked the usual questions," she wrote in *The Catholic Worker* — "how long I had known him, if he stated his position as c.o. or pacifist, whether or not he believed in defending himself. One of my answers offended him, because he pulled back his jacket and displayed the holster of a gun, and said 'I believe in defending *myself*.' I could not but think 'How brave a man, defending himself with his gun against us unarmed women and children hereabouts.'"

By the mid-1950s, Dorothy Day's FBI file bulged with several hundred pages. The FBI concluded that Dorothy was "either consciously or unconsciously being used by Communist groups. From our experience with her it is obvious that she maintains a very hostile and belligerent attitude toward the Bureau and makes every effort to castigate the Bureau whenever she feels inclined to do so." FBI Director J. Edgar Hoover personally added a note to her file, stating that Dorothy Day was "a very erratic and irresponsible person." Nevertheless, Dorothy was never arrested or questioned before the House Un-American Activities Committee in Congress, as were so many others during the McCarthy era. Despite her FBI file, Senator McCarthy never seemed especially concerned with her activities.

With the end of World War II, civilization had entered a terrifying new age. Nations were now equipped with atomic weapons that could destroy entire cities and leave behind a poisonous cloud of radioactive fallout. In the United States, government leaders urged the people to be prepared in the event of a nuclear war. Dorothy saw such "preparedness" as a menace to world peace, and she called on Americans to protest.

One dedicated protester, Ammon Hennacy, joined the Catholic Worker movement in 1952. The first time Dorothy met him, he asked her, "What jails have you been in and how long did you serve?" He told her proudly that he had spent several years in prison for evading the draft during the First World War. He also opposed paying federal income tax — although he earned so little money each year that this was seldom an issue in his own life. Since so much tax money supported the military, Ammon believed that all pacifists should be tax resisters.

Ammon Hennacy was often boastful and irritating. Although he called himself a Christian, he claimed that the Catholic Church was among the most evil institutions on earth. But he was an ardent pacifist who truly lived according to his beliefs. Dorothy sometimes told the Catholic Workers to "do as he does, not as he says."

Almost from the beginning, Ammon was in love with Dorothy. She had lived without romance ever since she had converted to Catholicism and left Forster Batterham. Now, at the age of fifty-five, she found herself being courted as though she were a schoolgirl by a rugged, energetic, outspoken man of sixty-two. Ammon sent her flowers, candy, and Valentines. When he was away (usually standing on a picket line or engaging in some other form of antiwar protest), he wrote to her every day. He begged her to marry him. "Each of us had to learn a lot the hard way," he said in one letter, "and I think we could easily have twenty years more now of good spade work to do together. . . . Right now I would like to embrace you and kiss you."

Dorothy respected Ammon deeply. But she wouldn't consider marriage, not even after he gave in to her wishes and became a Roman Catholic. Nevertheless, they remained close friends for more than a decade.

In January of 1952, Harper and Row published *The Long Loneliness,* Dorothy Day's autobiography. The title, she explained, came from Tamar's comment about her intense loneliness as the mother of young children. Dorothy realized that she herself had struggled with a sense of loneliness all her life, ever since that day when she had wandered off as a child and raced home in terror. Loneliness was an inevitable part of being human. The only escapes were life in community — the sort of life that the Catholic Worker movement tried to encourage — and a reliance upon God. Human friends might come and go, but God was always there.

In 1955, New York City launched a civil defense program to prepare its citizens for possible enemy air raids. When sirens sounded, everyone in the city was required by law to take shelter. Time after time for the next six years, Dorothy was involved in civil defense protests. When the sirens wailed, she and her fellow protesters sat in a park or walked up and down the sidewalk carrying placards. On several occasions she was arrested and given a suspended sentence. Once she spent ten days in jail, where, she wrote in *The Catholic Worker,* she had "a perfectly happy time."

During the 1950s, Dorothy was excited by the growing movement for civil rights among African-Americans in the South. She had long been distressed over the injustices against blacks under segregation. The African-American leader Martin Luther King, Jr. impressed her as a man of profound Christian commitment.

In the spring of 1957, Dorothy visited an integrated Christian commune near Americus, Georgia. The commune was somewhat similar to the Catholic Worker farms, and she was fascinated by what she saw. Many people in the nearby town were distressed because blacks and whites were living and working together, in violation of the state's written and unwritten laws. The commune had received threatening letters and phone calls, and the members feared that violence would erupt at any moment.

Every night, one member of the commune sat watch in a car in front of the farmhouse. One evening, fifty-nine-year-old Dorothy volunteered for watch duty. As she waited in the parked station-wagon, she heard tires screech toward her. She ducked down an instant before a shower of bullets shattered the window beside her.

Dorothy Day had been jeered for her beliefs. She had spent time in prison because of her moral convictions. Now, for the first time, her commitment to social justice had nearly cost her her life.

CHAPTER 11

The Challenge of Change

In 1960, Dorothy visited Chicago on a speaking tour. For the first time in more than forty years she walked along Cottage Grove Avenue and gazed up at the apartment where she had lived as a child. "The old flat still had its room with one window looking out to the lake," she wrote, "where my sister and I used to draw pictures and write stories and dress our dolls."

At sixty-three, Dorothy had started to look back over the past, remembering old times and reflecting upon the choices she had made. Some friends who had once been estranged by her religious conversion had begun to drift back into her life. Among them was Peggy Baird, the fun-loving artist with whom Dorothy had gone to Occoquan Prison. In 1963, Peggy's husband died, leaving her almost penniless. Dorothy invited her to move into the New York house of hospitality, and she was delighted when Peggy accepted. Peggy reveled in the sense of community that she found in the Catholic

Worker household. In 1968, shortly before her death, she became a Roman Catholic.

Although she often found herself looking back, Dorothy remained as involved as ever in the world around her. In 1960, several new young *Catholic Worker* reporters wrote about the Communist revolution in Cuba. Dorothy still opposed Communism because it rejected Christianity. But she explained in the paper that she was sympathetic with the Cuban Communists because she believed they were sincerely trying to help the poor. Some readers criticized her position, pointing out that the Cuban revolution had been a war of terrible bloodshed. How could Dorothy Day, a committed pacifist, approve of Fidel Castro and his firing squads? Dorothy acknowledged that she didn't approve of the violence which had accompanied the changes in Cuba. Yet Cuba was a Catholic country, and even Fidel Castro was a Roman Catholic. She hoped and believed that the revolution would succeed.

By 1962, the U.S. government had forbidden Americans to visit Cuba. Nevertheless, Dorothy managed to travel there, using a visa she obtained from the Czechoslovakian embassy. The experience impressed her deeply. "You cannot imagine how the Cuban Catholics to whom I spoke welcomed our message," she wrote to a friend. "I felt greatly reassured that I had done the right thing to come."

In 1964, the Catholic Worker sold Peter Maurin Farm, its property on Staten Island. Like most of the previous farming communes, it had never been very successful. With the money it had gotten for the farm, the Worker bought a twenty-five-room house in Tivoli, New York. The rambling old building stood on a bluff with a magnificent view of the Hudson River and the Catskill Mountains. The Tivoli property was purchased not as a working farm but as a center for retreats and conferences. During the 1960s, as the United States slid deeper and deeper into war in the southeast Asian nation of Vietnam, the Catholic Worker hosted a series of annual "Pax Tivoli Conferences" on world peace.

Concern for world peace sent Dorothy and a delegation of other Catholic Workers to the Vatican in Rome in 1965. The group hoped to urge the Vatican Council to issue a strong antiwar statement, giving Church sanction to conscientious objectors and calling for a ban on nuclear weapons. To Dorothy's sorrow, their mission met with little success.

While she was in Rome, Dorothy joined a ten-day fast to draw public attention to worldwide hunger. "It seemed to me that I had very special pains," she wrote later. "They were certainly of a kind I have never had before, and they seemed to pierce to the very marrow of my bones when I lay down at night." But when she thought of the starving millions in the world, she considered the fast "a small offering of sacrifice, . . . a few loaves and fishes. May we try hard to do more in the future."

The Vietnam War aroused little of the patriotic fervor

that Dorothy had found so distressing during World War II. Now, thousands of voices protested America's involvement in a conflict that seemed cruel, wasteful, and utterly unnecessary. Young people from all over the country attended the Pax Tivoli conferences, often hitchhiking to get there. One Catholic Worker, Eileen Egan, described the 1969 conference, which was based on the theme of nonviolence: "The whole group linked hands and began dancing on the lawn, turning in ever-widening circles until the lawn was a mass of moving people." But the conference was not all singing and dancing. Most of the time was spent in serious discussion and soul-searching. "With [Dorothy Day] always with us," Egan wrote, "we seem[ed] to achieve a heightened sense of community and commitment to peace."

Dorothy was thrilled as more and more priests and other church officials spoke out against the war. At last the Catholic Church was taking the lead, showing its members the way to meaningful social action. Two priests, Daniel and Philip Berrigan, led a series of protests at military installations around the country. The Berrigan brothers became heroes of the growing peace movement, inspiring thousands of young men to burn their draft cards and refuse to go into combat. With many of their followers, the Berrigans went to jail for their actions.

Throughout the turbulent 1960s, Dorothy strongly supported all forms of nonviolent protest against the war. She was appalled, however, when a young Catholic Worker took his own life to dramatize the horrors of the Vietnam conflict. Late in 1965, Roger LaPorte stood on the sidewalk in front of the United Nations building, doused himself with kerosene, and set his body ablaze.

Dorothy had never known LaPorte, though he had often been at the house on Chrystie Street. Certainly she had never encouraged him to make such a sacrifice in the name of peace. It was the love of life that had led to her conversion; the affirmation of life was the basis of all her work. Yet in the public outcry after LaPorte's death, many held Dorothy Day responsible. News reporters, church officials, and even some student protesters accused her of leading Roger on with her call for personal action. She was shocked and hurt by the anger directed toward her.

Since its beginnings, the Catholic Worker had been nourished by the commitment of young people who wanted to create a better world. But the youth rebellion that swept the nation during the 1960s was broader than the civil-rights and antiwar movements. Much of this upheaval was a challenge to authority and time-honored values. Young people explored the limits of personal freedom by experimenting with drugs and sex. Dorothy had little patience with or sympathy for the "hippies" who drifted to the Catholic Worker. They had no respect for the Catholic Church, for rules, or, it sometimes seemed to her, for themselves. Their attitude toward life appeared to be "If it feels good, do it." Their behavior appalled her, and she prayed for their salvation. In a period of near despair she wrote,

There is an element of the demonic in the air we breathe these days. Letters come daily from parents who flee the cities with children to escape, and evil is everywhere in the guise of sex and drugs, and words — "beautiful" — "love" — the "new family," etc. Much lying and deceit, self-justification — an arrogant taking over, a contempt for the old people, or tradition. They demand support, other people's work, to enable themselves to keep going. If refused, the ugly face of hate and violence is revealed, to subside into silent pride, arrogance, once more. "We know what we are doing. We are building a new order." What a parody of what we ourselves are trying to do. Self-discipline, self-denial, voluntary poverty, manual labor, washing the feet of others — they taunt us with all these things, oblivious to every need around them outside of their own circle, their own age group. . . . My heart aches for them, they are so profoundly unhappy. Their only sense of well-being comes from sex and drugs, seeking to be "turned on" to get high, to reach the heights of awareness, but [they are] steadily killing the possibility of real joy.

O God, come to my assistance. Lord, make haste to help us. Lord, hear my prayer. Let my cry come to Thee. In Thee have I hoped; let me never be confounded. All I have on earth is Thee. What do I desire in heaven beside Thee? And that "they" should have Thee, find Thee, love Thee too, those you have given us, sent to us, our children. May they cry out for the living God. . . . Let them seek and find the way, the truth, the light.

It had always been Dorothy's policy to accept anyone who came to the house of hospitality, no matter how disruptive or unpleasant that individual might be. Anyone who came for shelter, she contended, was a member of the family in Christ and could not be turned away. But one day she violated her own cherished rule. She grew so furious with a group of young people who were living in Catholic Worker apartments that, in a burst of temper, she threw them all out. For years afterward, Catholic Workers recalled the episode as "the Dorothy Day Stomp."

In the aftershocks following this explosion, Dorothy wrote sadly of these young people adrift: "It is a complete rebellion against authority, natural and supernatural, even against the body and its needs. . . . This is not reverence for life. It is a great denial. It is more resembling nihilism than the great revolution they think they are furthering."

The Catholic Church, too, was undergoing changes that Dorothy often found dismaying. Many of the priests who attended Catholic Worker retreats and conferences wore ordinary street clothes instead of the traditional costume. They lounged about casually with the young people, as though they were afraid to be figures of authority. Some of these men eventually left the priesthood because they wanted to marry, or because they had begun to question their faith.

One change, however, met with Dorothy's unqualified approval. She was delighted when the Catholic Church abandoned the traditional Latin Mass and began to conduct services "in the vernacular" — that is, in the language of its parishioners. She hoped that some disaffected young people would find new meaning in the Church liturgy when they heard the sacred words spoken in a language they could understand.

But even Dorothy's own daughter was no longer a practicing Catholic. Life had not been easy for Tamar. Her marriage to David Hennessy had never been smooth. For years the Hennessys had lived in virtual poverty. Dorothy had tried to help as much as she could, but she had often felt that David resented her interference. At last, after the birth of their ninth child, David had experienced a nervous breakdown and had been forced to leave the family.

Despite these difficulties, Dorothy had managed to remain very close to her daughter. Even during Tamar's most troubled times, Dorothy had found consolation with her and the children. "You alone do not make demands on me," she wrote to Tamar in 1969, "but welcome me when I come and do not reproach me. You do not know how grateful I am for that. You are a real comfort to me always."

The world was changing very swiftly, in ways Dorothy had never imagined possible. She needed all of the comfort she could find.

CHAPTER 12

The End of the Pilgrimage

On an August day in 1973, Dorothy Day stood in the sun beside Cesar Chavez, head of the United Farm Workers Union. She had traveled to California's San Joaquin Valley for a massive demonstration, calling for more humane working conditions in the fields and for the right of farm workers to unionize. More than one thousand people were arrested during the demonstration, and Dorothy Day was among them. She spent nearly two weeks in a California jail. "If it weren't a prison," she told reporters wryly, "it would be a nice place to rest."

Dorothy Day's picture appeared in newspapers all across the country. Journalists described her as a gallant old lady who had devoted her life to the oppressed. But in the photographs she looked frail and tired. The burden of her seventy-five years seemed to be bearing down upon her.

That visit to California was the last major trip

Dorothy ever made. During the 1970s, as her health failed and her energy faded, she turned down most speaking engagements. To one friend who asked her to deliver a lecture she wrote apologetically, "No speaking anywhere this year. I've talked too much and too long. Don't want to be a 'garrulous old woman.' Holy silence. But you see [I am] garrulous even [in] this note to say thank you."

When she walked for even a block, Dorothy had to stop, gasping for breath. Haste and excitement left her trembling. If she caught a cold, she took weeks to recover. Doctors told her that she had hardening of the arteries and an enlarged heart. Generally she tried to play down her illness, and she referred to her spells of weakness as "attacks of the flu."

Dorothy still wrote articles for *The Catholic Worker*. But she had relinquished most of her other responsibilities within the movement. She spent most of her time at the house in Tivoli, where she had private quarters on the top floor. "I'm living a life of leisure," she wrote to a friend. "Sometimes I feel like a relic, treasured and pampered and spoiled 'rotten' as my mother used to say. I wish you could see the luxury in which I live — large room and private bath. So much space it becomes a dumping ground. Where is my voluntary poverty? Two five-shelf bookcases crammed with books, good and bad. Everyone is always giving me things of beauty. So I sometimes think that in addition to running a library, I am in a museum." To

Dorothy, who had restricted so much of her life to bare necessities, one room, two bookcases, and a bathroom of her very own seemed the height of luxury indeed.

Although she reigned in her domain upstairs, Dorothy was often distressed by the atmosphere at the Tivoli house. There was little change in the trend that had dismayed her so much during the 1960s. The young people who were drawn to the Catholic Worker movement in the 1970s had little sense of a religious vocation. They avoided Mass and evening services, and they even squirmed uncomfortably when the older members of the community prayed before meals. They played loud music with a thundering beat, and they plastered the walls with posters of rock stars. "I'm considered an ancient old fogey," she told a friend in a letter, "and the more praise given me by the press, the more the young edge away from me. . . . You can imagine the kind of desolation I feel. . . . I have to learn daily over and over not to judge. But how not to?" The youth of the 1970s knew a sense of community, but it was based on their rejection of rules and authority. In the name of freedom, Dorothy felt, young people turned away from everything the Catholic Church had to offer.

The Catholic Church, too, was changing. "Certain prayers of the Mass, old and beautiful, have been dropped," Dorothy lamented, "and the [statues of the] saints to whom the people address themselves in their loneliness and sorrow have been moved to the back of the church, when they have not been moved down to the basement." In most Church matters, Dorothy was deeply conservative. She didn't believe that women should be ordained as priests, and she held firmly with the Church's stand against birth control and abortion. She feared that the thoughtless younger generation was constantly whittling away the tenets that made the Church strong.

When everything around her seemed to be crumbling, Dorothy still found solace in the Bible. As she had done since the early years of her conversion, she began each morning with a reading from the Psalms. She meditated upon the ideas which she considered her "philosophy of life," that God was the grounding, origin, destiny, and model for human living, as revealed in his son Jesus Christ. Christ's example affirmed and reaffirmed her convictions about pacifism, the sanctity of human life, and the redeeming power of love.

In her final years, Dorothy's life revolved around the people she had been closest to in the past. She and her sister, Della, visited as often as they could and kept up a lively correspondence. Dorothy also remained close to her brother John and to his wife, Tessa. In one letter, which she wrote when she was in her late seventies, she thanked Tessa once more for the hospitality she had shown to Peter Maurin when he had arrived at the apartment on Fifteenth Street more than forty years before.

Another old acquaintance who reappeared in Dorothy's life was Forster Batterham. They had never lost touch completely. Forster had always helped with

Tamar's financial support when she was a child, and he and Dorothy shared an abiding concern for their daughter's happiness. As they both grew older, the bond between them was renewed. In 1973, fighting a battle with cancer, Forster turned to Dorothy for emotional support. "My dear daughter's father has had six operations and is feeling low," Dorothy wrote. "He likes to see me hobble in and out with a cane. I am so happy he hangs onto me."

In 1976 Dorothy gave her last public address at the Catholic Eucharistic Congress in Philadelphia. She had been asked to speak on the role of women in the Church. Instead she talked about God's love as it is manifest in all creation. "My conversion began at a time when the material world began to speak in my heart of the love of God," she told her audience. "The Church taught me the crowning love of the life of the spirit." The date was August 6, and Dorothy reminded her listeners of the American bombs that had fallen on Hiroshima, Japan, thirty-one years before. "God gave us life, and the Eucharist to sustain our life," she said. "But we have given the world instruments of death in inconceivable magnitude."

In her old age, Dorothy was chosen to receive many honorary degrees and awards. Some she refused because she was too ill to travel to the necessary ceremonies. But one honor moved her very deeply. On her eightieth birthday, New York's Cardinal Terence Cook presented her with a special greeting from Pope John Paul II. The Catholic Church could offer no greater expression of its appreciation for her years of service and devotion.

In 1979 the house at Tivoli was sold, and Dorothy moved back into New York City. In 1976 the Catholic Worker had opened Maryhouse, a shelter for homeless women on New York's East Third Street. There Dorothy had private quarters, removed from the hubbub of the rest of the house. It was at Maryhouse that Dorothy spent most of her final years. Generally she passed her time in her room, reading, writing letters, and entertaining visitors.

From her window, Dorothy looked out upon a block of crowded tenements. Puerto Rican and African-American children played on the sidewalks, and teenagers lounged on the corner, looking for something to do. At one end of the block the notorious motorcycle gang, the Hell's Angels, had its headquarters. Day and night, young men on motorcycles roared beneath Dorothy's window. Dorothy had spent most of her years amid the poverty of the city. Perhaps it was only fitting that she should live out her final days with the noise and dirt and teeming life of East Third Street.

During the last years of her life, Dorothy endured many losses. Her beloved sister Della died. One of Tamar's sons was killed in a car accident. And on a November afternoon in 1980, the staunch Catholic Worker Stanley Vishnewski died of a sudden heart attack. With his last breath he managed to joke, "It must have been the Catholic Worker soup I had."

Two weeks later, on the evening of November 29, Dorothy Day died peacefully. She was eighty-three years old. Tamar, her daughter and confidante, was with her when she passed away.

Three days later, on December 2, hundreds of people crowded into Nativity Catholic Church a few short blocks from Maryhouse to attend Dorothy Day's funeral. Several of her grandchildren led the funeral procession. They were followed by Tamar, Forster, and Dorothy's brother John. The church was filled with friends from the Catholic Worker movement and with men, women, and children from the neighborhood. Many knew Dorothy only as a legend, the woman who had dedicated her life to the relief of human suffering through the action of Christian love.

As a special honor, Cardinal Cook appeared to say a few words of blessing over Dorothy's body. Just as he began to speak, a gaunt, ragged man broke from the crowd and rushed toward the coffin. His clothes were dirty, his hair was long and tangled, and his eyes were wild. As the mourners stared, he bent low over the coffin, muttering words that no one could understand. Then, as abruptly as he had come, he melted back into the crowd. It was as though he had arrived to say farewell for all of the homeless, tormented people whom Dorothy Day had helped throughout her long life of service.

Dorothy Day was buried at the Cemetery of the Resurrection on Staten Island, not far from the place where her fisherman's cottage once stood. Overhead, gulls circle and cry, bringing her messages from the sea.

EPILOGUE

A Legacy of Love

E arly in the morning, as the February winds whine along the busy city streets, a crowd of men and women gathers outside St. Joseph's House on East First Street. They are old and young, black and white and every shade in between. Some mutter to themselves; some stand stoically, gazing at the pavement. Nearly all of them look tired, battered by the harshness of life.

Inside, St. Joseph's House is warm, and the fragrance of fresh coffee fills the air. A smiling young man greets each guest with a friendly "Good morning!" Two young women hurry back and forth, serving coffee and hot rolls. The guests begin to relax. They settle at tables in the dining room, and soon everyone is talking at once. People complain about the weather, argue over politics, make predictions about the coming baseball season. The words don't really matter. The important part is that they are in a safe place, removed from the bleakness and turmoil of the world outside.

135

Two blocks north, on East Third Street, a priest says Mass in the auditorium at Maryhouse. Among the worshipers are two dozen homeless women, many of them newly released from psychiatric hospitals. Some bow their heads in prayer, and a few nod to sleep as the solemn words of the liturgy flow around them.

Out on the street, two college students shout, "Read *The Catholic Worker!* A penny a copy!" Most passersby keep walking without a glance in their direction. But now and then someone pauses, digs for a penny, and takes a copy of the paper. It is filled with news of peace demonstrations, of aid to war refugees, of food drives to help the victims of famine around the world.

The Catholic Worker movement has changed little since it began with Dorothy Day and Peter Maurin in 1933. It continues to draw young people eager to help those in need, to battle the world's injustices, to serve humanity in the spirit of Christian love. It continues to offer food, shelter, and compassion to the forgotten men and women of the city's ugliest slums. The newspaper is still a call to personal action in the name of Christ.

In the mid-1990s, about one hundred Catholic Worker farms and houses of hospitality are scattered across the United States and throughout the world — in Mexico, Canada, Great Britain, Australia, and New Zealand. Each is a community in its own right, appealing for its own funds, finding its own way. Yet all of them share a commitment to the principles that

Dorothy Day expressed in her writings, her lectures, and her life.

Dorothy Day, the political radical who turned to God, remains the guiding force behind the Catholic Worker movement. Cynics have argued that all her love and dedication never changed the world; human beings are as greedy and lost as they ever were. But through the lesson of her own actions, Dorothy Day opened a path that thousands of others have followed. As her friend Father Daniel Berrigan wrote of her, "The simple task, the one practically everyone boggled at or bowed out of, this she would do. . . . Her politics stemmed from a command that she heard proclaimed from some-one of no time or place, of every time and place, 'Blessed are the peace-makers, blessed are the poor in spirit. What you do for the least of these you do for me.'"

My Sources for This Book

I would like to take this opportunity to thank Philip Runkel, archivist with the Dorothy Day Papers at Marquette University Library, Milwaukee, Wisconsin, for his generous assistance and support during my writing of this book. He was always willing to answer questions and search out the odd fact, and his review of the manuscript proved invaluable.

The following books by and about Dorothy Day have also been extremely useful:

Coles, Robert. *Dorothy Day: A Radical Devotion*. Reading, Mass.: Addison-Wesley, 1987.

Coles explores the evolution of Dorothy Day's philosophy, drawing upon a series of in-depth interviews conducted near the end of her life.

————. *A Spectacle unto the World: The Catholic Worker Movement*. New York: Viking, 1973.

This history of the Catholic Worker movement is enhanced by photographs taken at St. Joseph's House and other houses of hospitality.

Cornell, Thomas C., and James H. Forrest, eds. *A Penny a Copy: Readings from "The Catholic Worker."* New York: Macmillan, 1968.

This anthology contains many of Dorothy Day's pieces, as well as articles and columns by other leading contributors to the paper.

Day, Dorothy. *From Union Square to Rome.* Silver Spring, Md.: Preservation of the Faith Press, 1938.

In an open letter to her brother, Dorothy Day traces her path from Socialist rebel to committed Roman Catholic.

———. *House of Hospitality.* New York: Sheed & Ward, 1939.

This is an account of the early years of the house of hospitality in New York.

———. *Loaves and Fishes.* New York: Harper & Row, 1963.

This book is a series of essays on life at the Catholic Worker houses of hospitality and farming communes, including vivid accounts of some of the people who played a crucial role in the movement.

———. *The Long Loneliness*. New York: Harper & Row, 1952.

Written with grace and eloquence, this is Dorothy's story in her own words. It traces her spiritual development from childhood through midlife.

———. *On Pilgrimage: The Sixties*. New York: Curtis, 1973.

This book continues Dorothy Day's story through the 1960s.

Ellsberg, Robert, ed. *By Little and by Little: The Selected Writings of Dorothy Day*. New York: Alfred A. Knopf, 1983.

This book gathers a generous sampling of Dorothy Day's work, including excerpts from her books, *Catholic Worker* columns, and articles from such periodicals as *The New Masses* and *Commonweal*.

Merriman, Brigid. *Searching for Christ: The Spirituality of Dorothy Day*. Notre Dame: University of Notre Dame Press, 1994.

Merriman explores the books, movements, and individuals that influenced Dorothy Day's spiritual growth.

Miller, William D. *Dorothy Day: A Biography*. New York: Harper & Row, 1982.

Written by a longtime friend and admirer, this biography is an essential tool for a thorough understanding of Dorothy Day's life and work.

————. *A Harsh and Dreadful Love: Dorothy Day and the Catholic Worker Movement*. New York: Liveright, 1973.

This is a comprehensive history of the Catholic Worker movement, rich with anecdotes about people and events.

————. *All Is Grace: The Spirituality of Dorothy Day*. Garden City, N.Y.: Doubleday, 1987.

Drawing upon letters, journals, and personal interviews, Miller examines the final years of Dorothy Day's life in terms of her work and religious vision.

O'Connor, June. *The Moral Vision of Dorothy Day: A Feminist Perspective*. New York: Crossroad, 1991.

O'Connor reviews Dorothy Day's life, work, and spirituality from a feminist viewpoint.

Roberts, Nancy L. *Dorothy Day and "The Catholic Worker."* Albany: State University of New York Press, 1984.

Roberts focuses on the history of *The Catholic Worker*, viewing the newspaper as a vehicle for social thought and spiritual teaching.

Suggestions for Further Reading

Church, Carol Bauer. *Dorothy Day: Friend of the Poor.* Minneapolis: Greenhaven Press, 1976.

This biography gives a good overview of Dorothy Day's life and work.

Collins, David R. *Dorothy Day: Catholic Worker.* Cincinnati: St. Anthony Messenger Press, 1981.

Written for younger readers, this is a brief account of Dorothy's life.

Farr, Naunerle. *The Roaring Twenties and the Great Depression.* New Haven: Pendulum Press, 1976.

A portrait of the two decades in which Dorothy Day formed her most important ideas and began her life's work.

Katz, William. *An Album of the Great Depression*. New York: Franklin Watts, 1978.

A description of the Great Depression, enriched with photographs and first-person narratives.

O'Grady, Jim. *Dorothy Day: With Love for the Poor.* Staten Island: Ward Hill Press, 1993.

This biography examines Day's life and work in detail, exploring her philosophy and spiritual quest as well as her dedication to social action.

Index

Baird, Peggy, 22, 23, 25,
  27, 44, 47, 49, 119-20
Batterham, Forster, 44-45,
  47, 49-50, 51, 53-54,
  55, 87, 116, 131-32, 134
Berrigan, Father Daniel,
  122, 137
Berrigan, Father Philip, 122
Bethune, Ade, 81

Catholicism/Catholic
  Church: changes in,
  125-26, 130-31; in
  Cuba, 120; in Mexico,
  58, 79-80; and social
  action, 57, 60, 67, 99,
  122; in Spain, 99; Vatican Council of, 121
Catholic Worker move-
  ment/activities: demon-
  strations, 79-80, 117-

18; farming communes,
  69, 86-89, 90-94, 109,
  113, 120-21, 136; FBI
  and, 114-15; houses of
  hospitality, 69, 78, 82-
  83, 85, 113-14, 125,
  133, 135-37; pacifist
  position of, 98-100,
  101, 102, 114, 117-18,
  121; philosophy of, 83-
  84, 95-96, 117, 136-
  37; retreat centers, 109-
  10, 120-21; spread of,
  85, 96, 136-37; volun-
  tary poverty in, 84-85
Catholic Worker, The, 72-75,
  80-81, 98-99, 129, 136;
  anti-war position of, 99-
  100, 102, 108; founding
  of, 69-72; personnel of,
  77-78, 100-101

Chavez, Cesar, 128
Civil rights movement, 118
Communism/Communist
    Party, 16, 38, 47, 59-
    60, 61, 72, 99, 114,
    120
Cook, Cardinal Terence,
    132, 134
Cowley, Malcolm, 44, 47,
    49, 119
Cowley, Peggy Baird. *See*
    Peggy Baird
Cuba, 120

Day, Della, 5, 10, 31, 74,
    97, 131, 133
Day, Donald, 12, 70, 98
Day, Dorothy: adolescence
    of, 9-14; and Bible read-
    ing, 6, 26-27, 28, 47,
    131; and Catholicism, 7,
    33, 41, 42, 51-54, 55,
    56, 57, 60, 66-67, 71,
    98, 130-31; childhood
    of, 1-9; and civil rights
    movement, 118; in col-
    lege, 15-20; death of,
    134; education of, 12,
    13-14, 15, 16, 18, 19;
    on fasts, 25-28, 121; and
    FBI, 114-15; illnesses of,
    54-55, 102, 121, 129;
    marriage of, 36-37; as
    nurse, 31-32, 35; as paci-

fist, 99, 100, 101, 115-
    16, 121, 122; in prison,
    24-28, 38-40, 118, 128;
    public addresses of, 95-
    96, 129, 132; romances
    of, 9-10, 34-36, 45-46,
    116-17; and Socialism,
    16, 19, 99; spiritual life
    of, 1-2, 6-8, 11, 13, 16-
    17, 26-27, 28, 30, 33-
    34, 41, 47-49, 57, 83-
    84, 104-6, 110, 131; and
    Vietnam War, 121-23;
    and women's issues, 23-
    24, 58
Day, Grace Satterlee, 4-5,
    9, 35, 98, 105
Day, John (brother), 9, 15-
    16, 59, 61, 70, 73, 74,
    97-98, 131, 134
Day, John (father), 2-3, 4,
    5, 8, 13, 19-20, 69, 98
Day, Sam, 5, 69-70, 98
Day, Tamar Teresa, 110-11,
    113, 117, 126, 133,
    134; adolescence of,
    103-4, 105; childhood
    of, 62, 68, 74, 91, 132;
    infancy of, 50-51, 52,
    53, 54, 58-59; marriage
    of, 106-7

Earthquake, San Francisco
    (1906), 1-2, 6, 13

Eleventh Virgin, The, 37, 42-43

Francis of Assisi, Saint, 68
From Union Square to Rome, 98

Great Depression, 59, 78, 100

Hand, Armin, 9-10
Hennacy, Ammon, 116-17
Hennessy, David, 104, 106-7, 110, 126
Hitler, Adolf, 80, 100
House of Hospitality, 98
Houses of hospitality: 69, 125, 136; on Charles Street, 79; on Chrystie Street, 113-14; on East Fifteenth Street, 78; on Mott Street, 81-82, 83, 100, 113; St. Joseph's House, 135; spread of, 85, 102, 136-37

International Workers of the World (IWW), 38

Kramer, Mae, 37-38, 39

Labor movement, 12, 16, 38, 59-60, 80, 128

LaPorte, Roger, 122-23
Long Loneliness, The (autobiography), 9, 37, 55, 117

McCarthy, Senator Joseph, 114, 115
Maryfarm (Easton, Pennsylvania), 90-94, 103, 104
Maryfarm (Newburgh, New York), 109-10
Maryhouse, 133, 136
Maurin, Peter, 61-65, 66-67, 68-69, 70, 71, 72-73, 75, 76, 80, 86-87, 88, 97, 107, 111-13, 131, 136
Mexico, 58-59, 74-75, 79-80
Moise, Lionel, 34-36, 37, 38, 41

Nuclear weapons, 108, 115-16, 121, 132

Occoquan prison, 24-28, 40
O'Neill, Eugene, 29-30

Pax Tivoli Conferences, 121, 122
Peter Maurin Farm, 113, 120-21
Porcelli, Julia, 77-78, 79

San Francisco Earthquake
of 1906, 1-2, 6, 13
Simons, Rayna, 18, 19, 20,
23
Socialism/Socialist Party,
16, 19, 21, 22-23, 50,
51, 99
Spanish Civil War, 99, 100

Teresa of Ávila, Saint, 50
Tobey, Barkley, 36-37

University of Illinois, 13-
14, 15, 19

Vietnam War, 121-22
Vishnewski, Stanley, 77,
83, 133

Women's suffrage, 23-24
World War I, 22, 29, 31, 49
World War II, 100, 102,
107-8, 114, 115